BUSES
Yearbook 1994

Edited by
Stewart J. Brown

IAN ALLAN
Publishing

CONTENTS

First published 1993

ISBN 0 7110 2154 6
Collector's edition: ISBN 0 7110 2214 3

All rights reserved. No part of this book may be reproduced
or transmitted in any form or by any means, electronic or
mechanical, including photocopying, recording or by any
information storage and retrieval system, without permission
from the Publisher in writing.

© Ian Allan Ltd 1993

Published by Ian Allan Ltd, Shepperton, Surrey; and printed
by Ian Allan Printing Ltd at their works at Coombelands in
Runnymede, England.

Cover:
**Trent Leyland National 513 (ACH 513T) basks in the
sunshine at Derby bus station in August 1992, shortly after
having undergone light refurbishing and repainting in
current livery. See 'Through the driver's eyes'.**
STEPHEN C. MORRIS

Back cover, upper:
**This Leyland Leopard, originally Shamrock & Rambler 3021
(REL 401R), was rebodied for Compass Bus, Wakefield, by
Plaxton in 1987 as KIB 6110. It is now South Yorkshire 69.
See 'Old buses never die . . .'.**
JOHN YOUNG

Back cover, lower:
**A new look in Bradford; illustrated by a Roe-bodied Leyland
Titan PD3A in the city centre, soon after the West Yorkshire
PTE takeover. See 'Flashback: 20 years ago'.**
STEWART J. BROWN

Previous page:
**Standard-wheelbase Olympians were purchased by Stagecoach
in 1992 with bodywork by Northern Counties and, as shown
here, Alexander. While the corporate livery makes it clear that
this is a Stagecoach group bus, the large fleetname leaves no
doubt which subsidiary is operating it.**
MURDOCH CURRIE.

THE SURVIVORS

Seven out of a batch of ten open-top Bristols, new
40 years ago, still survive. **John G. Lidstone**
investigates

'They're *what*?' I said. 'All o' these will be off the road for scrap at the end of the month,' replied the conductor. Suddenly a sunny afternoon became very cloudy as the sense of impending loss sank in. We crowled up the steep Grand Drive Hill in Leigh. 'One's gone already.' He was right, too; Southend's Beadle-bodied Leyland PD1 NVX311 had been sold to a buyer in South Carolina and Clacton's LEV920 had replaced it, notably without allocation plates or proper blinds and full of cobwebs. Not proper stuff at all as Southend's PD1s were always spotless. Despite as many rides as pocket-money would allow, the end came all too quickly. So quickly that I didn't even notice if the cobwebs had gone or not. Well, almost; of Eastern National's dozen Leyland Titan PD1 open-toppers, the oldest, ex-City Coach Co Alexander-bodied PD1/1 LEV917 has been superbly preserved unusually after several semi-world tours with its initial purchaser. The rest simply vanished to scrapyards and never saw any of them ever again.

Feverish speculation as to what would replace them followed. Bristol FLFs I wondered? No, they're far too new. Bristol Ks? No, same age as the PD1s.

They'd never be Bristols anyway as they're standard and open-toppers usually aren't. Constructively, my pencils drew an ex-Moores Guy Arab/Massey in open-top form; it looked nice. They didn't get converted either.

Just a few weeks later, my father dutifully brought our car to a controlled stop (thinking I'd had some kind of spasm) for I'd just glimpsed a strange apparition through the half-open doors of Eastern National's Prittlewell Works. In an instant it was clear — the new open-toppers ousting the 1947-9 Leylands were -1953 Bristols! There was KSW5G WNO 483 with roof lopped, panels stripped off and with a chunky-looking new upper saloon windshield taking shape. Confirmation came when Gordon Watts' Fleet News in *Buses Illustrated* December 1965 recorded 'To replace the open-toppers, several KSW5Gs are being converted to open-top, viz: 2378-87 (with WNO registrations.)'

As delivered: WNO483 at Colchester in October 1953.
G.R. MILLS

Being converted: the same bus at Prittlewell works in 1965. It was destroyed by fire in this shed in 1981.
T. COUGHLIN.

My heart sank. Slow, plodding old 5LW-engine Bristols abounded in Southend. Their saving grace was that fully-laden specimens would entertainingly boil over quite regularly outside my parents' house after the half-mile second-gear slog up from Leigh station on those long, hot summer days (EN's KSWs didn't have radiator fans fitted even from new). Some would even show Extra Relief Service and would then make it into my notebook twice that day. I was taken aback that such feeble machines should oust my quiet and melodious six-cylinder PD1s which *never* boiled

Santa's special: WNO481 reverts to a covered top for Christmas 1966.
G. R. MILLS.

...p. Seemed daft to me. I was convinced they'd never make it up Grand Drive with a good load and I was sure they would regret it. I felt better straight away.

Before all you Bristol fans jam the Ian Allan switchboard, that was 1965 and as a young schoolboy had no way of knowing that the WNOs would become far better friends than the PD1s, or that I would even drive them myself (not once boiling over, despite continued lack of fans). Most remarkable of all is that I couldn't have been more wrong; the WNOs have become the most enduring, widely-travelled and perhaps popular of any batch of KSWs built. 1993 saw their 40th year with seven of the ten still active and this is a tribute to some very good friends.

Their pedigree? Well, Westcliff-on-Sea and Eastern National's last exposed-radiator Bristols were WNO 472-9 and WNO 480-5 respectively. New in 1953, they were united in the Eastern National fleet in 1954. All 87 KSWs supplied had lowbridge layout, but the WNOs featured the less-common and unpopular staggered version of the lowbridge pattern. Each upper-saloon seat (in groups of four) was positioned slightly behind its left-hand neighbour. The idea was supposedly an improvement, but the antiquated sunken gangway concept died a swift death with the onward march of the Lodekka in the next year, 1954. Years of unpopularity with conductors no doubt made them top choice for conversion to highbridge-layout open-toppers.

So, back to the future — well, 1965 anyway. Not to be outdone, Chelmsford (Head Office) workshops

beavered away converting WNO480 at the same time as WNO483 at Prittlewell, in October. Prittlewell's certainly won points for feet of coach trim used, also for rear destination and number displays but Chelmsford's won hands down for good looks, producing the most handsome conversions.. Slightly less trim and only a rear number made them look neater, with a superbly styled windshield that complemented the classic Eastern Coachworks lines. WNO475/9-81-4 thus benefited at Chelmsford, the uglier sisters from Prittlewell being WNO474/8/82/3/5. Head-banging sunken gangway intrusions in their lower saloon ceilings had at last gone, but the antique plastic-covered ex-PD1 seats didn't achieve much for looks or comfort. The last two conversions, WNO479/81, emerged only just in time for the 1966 season in May, probably with paintwork still hardening on the way to that annual open-top bus rally, more properly known as The Derby at Epsom Downs!

WNO472/3/6/7 kept their roofs and were appropriately amongst the last KSWs pensioned-off in 1971. Just one escaped the scrapman briefly — WNO476, which appeared in the On the Buses films as Luxton & District Bus Co's No 2675 in all-over red. It miserably ended its film career by being broadsided by an ex-United Counties KSW in a rather spirited depot incident.

The new open-toppers quickly proved themselves useful for all types of special events. City of London Polytechnic regularly hired two for the annual London-Brighton HCVC run, where they would rub shoulders with ex-BH&D Bristols for an afternoon. The Derby would see all of them scattered around the enclosures, featured in TV coverage each year.

Service support: with blanked-out windows, WNO485 was used as a tree-lopper.
JOHN G. LIDSTONE.

Close encounter: WNO484 ran into a house in Eastwood in 1973. It was rebuilt and was still in regular service 20 years later.
JOHN G. LIDSTONE

Colchester United FC would be glad of one from time to time as would newly-weds of company employees. They occasionally appeared in winter as driver trainers or depot runabouts, often well away from their summer homes; at Christmas, the Co-op regularly hired one for a Santa Special between Colchester and Clacton, carrying a built-up top-deck Santa's Grotto. WNO474/85 were even dressed up as galleons, complete with firing cannons to be seen on TV chasing one another around for a Michael Bentine film! Early signs of staff-affection came when Southend's gained names such as *Rob Roy* (474), *Rocket Racer* (479), *Hot Rod* (480) and *Apache* (483), carried on bonnet-top stickers. Seafront services in both Southend and Clacton had passed their peak even in 1966, so sadly the new open-toppers only remained in stock complete for just two seasons. Strangely, their slow, periodic disposal was to prove the secret of their success.

First to go were Clacton's WNO481/2 in January 1968 to Eastern Counties, thus becoming the only two never to work at Southend. Initially together at

Below:
National style: WNO475 in corporate NBC colours, covering for a failed Southend Corporation PD3 in 1974.
JOHN G. LIDSTONE.

elixstowe, 482 went to Cromer for 1969/70 and 481 moved to Great Yarmouth for 1970. Both were sold in May 1971 — after Derby Day. WNO481 then achieved fame as the psychedelic Wings Bus, used by Beatles star Paul McCartney to tour Europe promoting his album *Wings over Europe*. Later with Tricentrol, it was repainted into a peculiar mustard/white livery, but I believe it never lost the yen for long-distance travel: I last encountered it *en route* for the Cannes Film Festival in May 1989 in a smart red/cream livery. WNO482 joined Cullings of Norwich as a publicity bus, but was soon in passenger use and making appearances for Norwich City Football Club. Its grey, yellow and cream livery gave way to white/red when taken over by Redcar of Norwich, but soon it passed to well-known auctioneers/removers Abels for disposal. They instantly took a shine to it and kept it! Smartly outshopped in pale/mid blue livery, Abels fitted it with a removable 'control tower' for conducting open-air events. Its Prittlewell screens could be refitted as required. As I write, in the last weeks of 1992, it has just been acquired by the Castlepoint Transport Museum, thus reunited with WNO475/8.

Meanwhile, WNO478 had been banished to Basildon — an uncompromising and landlocked New Town with no inclination for open-top KSWs. During its spell there as a driver training, a group of busmen became fond of it, cherishing it some ten years before the trend became popular. It gained an attractive non-standard livery with green band — bland all-over cream with green wings and radiator was the norm. Withdrawn in December 1971, it was sold for preservation to the same group, the embryo Eastern National Preservation Group. It has now been with ENPG longer than its entire career with EN and is no stranger overseas, having made many forays to Continental Europe to Dutch rallies, German beer festivals and even Swiss mountains. The latter proved too much for the perennial boiling problem, so it now sports a radiator fan and can happily attack the longest drag and keep cool!

During the 1970s, Eastern National was frequently unable to staff its scheduled operations and so these very Tilling products found themselves based uncomfortably amongst very municipal Massey-bodied Leyland Titans on seasonal hire to Southend Corporation Transport. SCT somehow always managed to operate services reliably that EN couldn't, so blue uniforms outnumbered green in their cabs for the decade.

WNO485, although newest, was next to go. After the 1968 season at Southend it was downgraded as a tree-lopper in sickly pale green/cream ancillary livery, ousting an ex-BH&D K5G. Gradually more battered year on year, it lasted five years before going for scrap.

Mastery of the KSW crash gearbox was a challenge that all SCT drivers attempted, most managed but some abjectly lost. Your writer (a seasonal SCT driver

Double-headed: Late running on the 1978 Southend Carnival Day brings two WNOs together at the Kursaal.
JOHN G. LIDSTONE.

Flag flying: WNO479, first prize winner at the 1982 carnival with NBC flags fluttering in the breeze.
JOHN G. LIDSTONE.

at the time) begs admission to the first category, having found the WNOs a delight to drive, with featherlight steering and no need to use the clutch except for pulling away from rest. A dream compared with heavy PD3s! For cold days, the Gardner 5LW heating system kept you warm. Once you prised it open and secured it, the opening windscreen kept you cool on hotter occasions, but also allowed the pilot to be peppered with flies, wasps, mosquitoes and, on Carnival days, various denominations of loose change The vacuum windscreen wiper would hiss and suck frantically (a real pain to stop once started) whilst the

Taking shape: wooden struts and sheets of paper as WNO480 is transformed into a mobile shoe.
JOHN G. LIDSTONE.

handbrake would merrily rattle about in the corner of the cab. The term floating cab always seemed apt for a KSW as cab and bonnet/radiator would dance about independently, water splashing out of the loose-fitting radiator cap at speed. Amusing diversions, these; the vacuum brakes had to be treated with care and respect, however, especially when taking over from a crew which had been *in extremis* to hand over their charge on time.

The management pen next struck off WNO474. A gearbox problem had seen it firmly relegated as spare bus during 1972, which was its last season. It became a tree-lopper and replaced battered sister WNO485 in January 1973. Ironically the first WNO in NBC colours, it was unfortunately drab all-over green and later unrelieved yellow. It was to be the company's last tree-topper and was scrapped in 1976.

Defying fate as WNOs often do, an accident was to actually secure the future of another of the clan. July 1973 saw WNO484 run out of control into a house at Eastwood on service 67 after catching the kerb. The bus won — the front of the house collapsed after it was dragged clear — but the battered bus never ran again. Sold for cannibalisation to South Wales Transport in August 1974, SWT quickly realised WNO's potential. Over the winter, parts were taken from an ex-United Welsh KSW6G and 22-year old 484 proudly inaugurated a new seafront service between Swansea City Centre and Limeslade in summer 1975. Outshopped in standard NBC red/white band livery and numbered 500, it gained silver/white for the Queen's Silver Jubilee in 1977, then reversed Skyrider white/red, later NBC white/green named *William Gammon* and, in 1992, pseudo-Eastern

National livery of cream/green band, but with black radiator and wings. Scheduled now to work its Limeslade run again in 1993, it became the last of the WNOs to see regular service. At 40 it has now outlived the three brand new convertible open-top VRTs that were expected to see *its* withdrawal!

By 1974 — still 20 years ago — the remaining four were already amongst the oldest buses in the entire National Bus Company. Eastern National had become quite proud of its veterans, which took on a new look that year in NBC white with green band beneficially added, rear displays and side fleetname wings removed. Carefully refurbished, even their radiator shells were polished and shone like new. They looked superb, a credit to their operator. Increasing staff difficulties meant their use became more sporadic, EN operations being largely confined to Clacton with SCT operating them in Southend.

Not to be put off, Southend Eastern National staff adopted WNO483 as a showbus in 1977 to rival Hadleigh depot's well known FLF. Over the years to 1981 it was steadily improved to quite an exceptional standard — equal to the best of our preserved buses. Very sadly, it became one case where WNO luck ran out. Four years' hard work saw 483 finally completed with brand new flooring (and even a temperature gauge on the dash to warn of the age-old boiling). After the Southend Torchlight Carnival in August 1981, there was no room at Southend, so it retired to

Above:
Sad end: WNO483 after the fire at Prittlewell.
JOHN G. LIDSTONE.

Left:
Top view: Abels, the East Anglian removals specialists, fitted a removable top deck cover to WNO482.
G. R. MILLS.

Prittlewell for the night — the same shed in which it had been converted back in 1965 but now a coach depot. Then, disaster struck: in two hours it was totally gutted by fire caused by mindless juveniles. Many tears were shed the following day by the volunteer staff whose efforts had been so cruelly turned into twisted and charred scrap.

1978 saw the first KSW-replacement open-topper, a former coach Lodekka. Very hastily cut down, it was a most unsatisfactory beast and rubbed shoulders unhappily with an apprehensive WNO479/80 that season. I had the honour of driving 479 on its historic last journey in Southend in September, complete with appropriate headboard. Thus the last ex-Westcliff-on-Sea psv also brought 25 years' unbroken WNO operation to an end.

Three more FLFs were crudely lopped for 1979 which displaced the WNOs at a stroke. Both were in store in summer 1981 — in Prittlewell. Withdrawn

Summer days: WNO475 on the sea front at Westcliff in 1977.
JOHN G. LIDSTONE

nd already with fleetnames crudely daubed over in dark green seat paint, they stood just feet from the magnificent showbus 483 as it burnt to the ground. Miraculously, both 479/80 escaped.

1982 saw our last two survivors blackened, filthy and dejected after the fire, but then WNO luck struck back. Suddenly they appeared at Southend depot in July for a clean-up. Clacton depot Sports & Social Club had asked to use one for the local Carnival procession prior to disposal. Southend's S&SC immediately took pity on poorly-looking 479 and so yet another new chapter in the WNO story began.

Southend driver Dave Wildish had both artistic eye and practical ability and quickly turned 479 into a papier mâché galleon *Explorer* complete with three masts (with sails) which took its height well over 20ft. It won well-deserved highly commended first prize at each event it attended. Although cheered by success, once stripped of all its paper and hardboard, its forlorn appearance struck Southend's staff once more. Over the pits she went for the full 483 treatment. Management now coughed, however, so the work was never fully completed.

Dave ensured 479 appeared in the 1983 carnival as *NSAS ENSC Starship*. It won first prizes again, but this time it was getting on for 20ft wide as the spacecraft had a sizeable wingspan!

For summer 1984, the intrepid pair were treated to a fresh coat of cream with green trim and hand-signwritten underlined fleetnames. WNO479 got itself banished to Basildon, still as landlocked as ever, so it became WNO480's turn for Carnival Capers. 1985 proved a vintage year, as the bus was completely unrecognisable beneath its disguise as *The Old Woman who Lived in a Shoe* – a gigantic 29ft boot. Driver's vision was quite appalling on this creation, as he had to peer through a tiny window in the said house. The toe of the boot was also some way in front of the dash ! 1986 saw it take on the shape of a Mississippi stern-wheeler, set off by some very enthusiastic costumes. As before, highly commended first prizes were the well-justified norm. Deregulation put paid to many niceties of the bus industry — sadly, one being these successful antics — which had not only boosted garage pride and raised money for charity, but also ensured that a KSW would reside at Southend each summer, even if not for passenger service.

1987 unexpectedly brought WNO479 back into regular use at Clacton on new service 300, managing to get itself prominently featured in a local picture postcard of the prom that year. WNO480 joined it for 1988, but 1989 saw the pair transferred to Hadleigh to operate merely as backups for the two Bristol VRT open-toppers (100 per cent spare coverage was never required in KSW days!). The VRTs had replaced the four FLFs, which in turn had supposedly replaced our KSWs. Amazingly, the duo now ran side-by-side on Essex County Council contracted service 67 on Southend seafront, won by EN in that year only. Appearances in service were very few, no enthusiasm being shown by the company. 1991 and 1992 saw both appear erratically on driver training from Chelmsford, private charter and special Wednesday afternoon vintage tours of the Tendring Hundred from Clacton, complete with live commentary from local guides. EN's southern area has now become Thamesway country, so 479/80 have been effectively barred from their traditional home area for good.

Well, that's the story — so far; rumour has it that Eastern National is planning to put one of 479/80 back in regular service at Clacton (hopefully minus cobwebs). Joking aside, here's hoping that this unique consecutive pair will remain together for many more years. As true veterans, they now evoke a long-gone era. Meanwhile, 484 lives on at Swansea. 475/8/82 are safely in preservation at Canvey and 481 is thought to be still on its continental wanderings — not bad really, seven out of ten at 40.

I'd like to thank Geoff Mills and the many friends at Eastern National's Southend depot who not only welcomed my interest in their open-toppers but also allowed me to take part in Carnival Capers each year.

Last run: WNO479 at Temple Sutton on 24 September 1978 for its last run, driven by the author, before withdrawal. It was returned to service in 1987.
JOHN G. LIDSTONE.

BRIDGEMASTER BLUNDER

The integral Bridgemaster was one of AEC's least
successful models. **Geoff Mills** illustrates a selection
of the 180 built.

The first two Bridgemasters had AEC 7.7-litre
AV470 engines. The second was painted in
Birmingham City Transport colours and after
a period as a demonstrator was purchased
by BCT. New in 1956, it was withdrawn by
Birmingham in 1969.
ALL PHOTOS BY GEOFF MILLS.

While production Bridgemasters had angular
Park Royal bodies, the early prototypes were
in fact handsome buses. This is a 1957 ex-
demonstrator, which spent most of its life
running for Barton Transport. Its Park Royal
body was of a style supplied to a number of
operators on conventional chassis.

A 1959 bus, one of six operated by Grimsby-Cleethorpes, shows just how different production vehicles looked. The Bridgemaster had rear air suspension and all but the first two were powered by AEC's 9.6-litre AV590 engine. This one was photographed in 1972.

Most early Bridgemasters had rear-entrance bodies, including six for Cardiff Corporation in 1960. These were 68-seaters and served the Welsh capital until 1972. They were unusual in being 27ft 8in long; most Bridgemasters were built to the then legal maximum length of 30ft.

This 1960 model, one of the first with forward-entrance bodywork, was built as a demonstrator and finished in the livery of Birmingham City Transport who, despite having bought an earlier Bridgemaster demonstrator, was an operator with few AECs and no lowheight or lowbridge buses. It was sold to Osborne of Tollesbury and is seen in Colchester in 1973. It was Osborne's second ex-demonstration Bridgemaster.

The Bridgemaster was one of the most oddly-proportioned products to be built by Park Royal, with its shallow windows and generally top-heavy frontal appearance. South Wales Transport, then part of the BET group, took five in 1960 and ultimately had 23 in its fleet. The plain red livery did not enhance the appearance of SWT's Bridgemasters.

Rotherham Corporation had a need for lowheight buses, and bought five Bridgemasters in 1960-61 to replace older side-gangway lowbridge 'deckers. Rotherham's livery did a little to disguise the model's uncompromising lines. Note the chock under the front wheel, attached to the driver's cab by a length of cord.

Below:

outhend Corporation was another municipal operator with a eed for lowheight buses and it received four Bridgemasters in 960 – but its next lowheight order specified Albion Lowlanders. he Bridgemasters were 76-seaters, a high carrying capacity for front-engined rear-entrance bus. They were sold in 1973 and ere Southend's last AEC double-deckers.

Bottom:

The Scottish Bus Group bought one Bridgemaster. This had in fact been ordered by Baxter's Bus Service of Airdrie which had been taken over by SBG subsidiary Scottish Omnibuses. The bus was delivered to Scottish Omnibuses in 1963 and ran for 10 years. It is seen in Edinburgh in 1971. The short window ahead of the door was an unusual feature.

Red Rover of Aylesbury bought this Bridgemaster in 1962 and followed it up with a forward-entrance example (a cancelled Baxter's order) in 1963. Both ran with Red Rover until 1977.

City of Oxford Motor Services, an enthusiastic AEC operator, bought 23 Bridgemasters. Its second batch were short-wheelbase 65-seaters, the only short Bridgemasters of forward-entrance layout. The body retained standard size windows, but with an unusually short side window at the front of the upper deck. They were new in 1963, the year Bridgemaster production ceased.

BODY STYLES – A TURN FOR THE BETTER?

Peter Rowlands maintains that the era since 1980 has brought the biggest change in bus styling for thirty years.

Bus styling seems to take for ever to evolve. This can be comforting in a way. Whatever changes you see in architecture or fashion, buses seem to go on looking basically the same. The Northern Counties-bodied Olympian you caught in Holborn last week looks very much like the Metrobus you saw there ten years ago. And it bears more than a passing resemblance to a Fleetline dating from ten years before that.

Yet this comfortable sense of continuity may not hold good for much longer. In the last ten years or so a whole range of new body styles has come breezing into the British bus industry, and recently the pace has quickened. Arguably we're seeing the biggest single outward development in bus design for 30 years — and one of only two or three fundamental style changes since we moved out of the era of the charabanc.

You don't have to look far for examples of the modern style. Among double-deckers, Optare's Spectra is the shining example. In the world of single-deckers there's the airy, angular Plaxton Verde; there's the trend-setting slope-screened Optare Delta; there's the fine-lined Dennis Dart from Duple (then Carlyle, then Marshall). They are all different from one another, they're all striking, and they all represent a major break from what went before.

Optare's trend-setting Delta, in service with United in Durham. ALL PHOTOS BY PETER ROWLANDS.

Why, when the bus industry is languishing in the doldrums, should styling be surging forward with such gusto? Paradoxically, one answer is that in previous decades, relative prosperity held back development. Giant operators like the National Bus Company were buying vehicles in large quantities, and above all they wanted uniformity. Who could blame the manufacturers if they simply kept on churning out what the customer demanded?

That's how it came about that the good old Bristol VRT double-decker, with its long-outmoded ECW body, was still being built at the start of the 1980s, using styling that dated back to World War 2. By the same token, London continued buying MCW Metrobuses by the 100, happy in the knowledge that its body design had much in common with the previous Leyland and Daimler Fleetlines.

It's only lately, with the industry in chronic decline, that manufacturers have been prompted to think hard about what buses should look like, and make efforts to woo their customers with advanced and attractive styling that breaks away from the past.

The trouble is that bus style has traditionally been influenced more by practicality than by appearance. Engineers want parts that are easy (and cheap) to replace; and they don't like new models that have nothing in common with the old. So it has been inevitable that bus styles have progressed by slow evolution rather than by radical change.

Besides, buses have an extremely long life in relation to other road vehicles. Cars tend to start looking dated within five years of their launch, whilst buses may well last three times as long. Bus stylists therefore tend always to look for timeless designs that won't age within a few years. And once they've found one (or think they have), why change?

Yet styling can and does have a real effect on attitudes to bus travel in the community at large. When it doesn't change from year to year, potential passengers — or let's call them customers — don't actually see the buses around them. Not unless they're

London's Metrobuses had body styling which had much in common with the previous generation of Fleetlines bodied by Park Royal and MCW.

enthusiasts, that is. So there's nothing visual to encourage non-users to become customers. What could be an important sale aid is sacrificed to practicality.

The explosion of new liveries in the 1980s was intended to break that particular mould, but in retrospect many of them now seem ill-conceived and extremely ephemeral. And underneath, the same old bus designs were still being used.

It's probably worth defining what is meant by 'style'. In this context it means the overall shape of the structure, along with the fine detail of execution. It means all those characteristics of the vehicle that distinguish it from others and endow it with a kind of personality of its own. Cars have this personality; so do many inanimate objects from buildings to hi-fi units. Buses certainly do, and if you don't recognise it you probably shouldn't be reading this in the first place.

On a bus, style means the width and depth of the windows; it means the thickness of the pillars; the shape of the front and rear domes and side covering; the size and texture of grilles; the basic proportions. It means, in a nutshell, the way in which individual components are combined to create an integrated whole.

So what were the styles of 1980? When you look at the buses of the period you find designs that were broadly unchanged from those of ten or 15 years before. Take the Northern Counties double-decker, for

The Selnec and Greater Manchester standard body set the pace in the 1970s. It developed into a new standard for Northern Counties, which continues in production in 1993. A GM Buses Metrobus, one of 30 bodied by Northern Counties, heads through Manchester's Piccadilly Gardens.

instance. The basics were more or less fixed with the establishing of Manchester's famous "Standards" in the early-1970s. But that design in turn was derived from Ralph Bennett's famous Bolton-style bus of the late-1960s. And its essentials went back to the contemporary designs of the day.

In other words, Northern Counties' 1980 standard double-decker had a clear lineage going back at least 15 years. As an alternative, you could opt for an East Lancs body, but that dated back more or less as far. Other double-deck body designs in production at the turn of the 1980s were those used on the MCW Metrobus (also a spiritual heir of the Bennett lineage) and the Leyland Titan, both now out of production.

Conceptually, the Titan body (like the ECW Olympian that followed it) was an uneasy mix of the existing ECW lines and the Bennett tradition — with high minded ergonomics thrown in for good measure. The result: a body which, like the camel, looked as if it had been designed by a committee, and arguably missed most of the marks it aimed for. Deep windows for downstairs passengers (lucky them), shallower ones upstairs. Inward sloping upper deck windows that must surely have come from a book on bus design by

The Titan body had deep lower-deck windows and a windscreen dictated by London Transport's preferences. This is a former Greater Manchester bus running for South Midland in 1988.

numbers; and a front dome with distinct ECW reminiscences. And to finish it all, an engine cowling that blocked off half of the lower rear window.

And this was supposed to be the dawning of a new era! Admittedly, as enthusiasts we may love these vehicles, but stylistically they can hardly be called ideal. The Leyland-group Olympian body that followed the Titan was cast very much in same mould, perpetuating the styling compromises inherent in the original.

The only real foretaste of the future at that time was Walter Alexander's R-type. This was launched at the turn of the 1980s, although it might have appeared even sooner but for the company's unyielding perseverance with its long-serving, rounded AL and AV series. The R-type brought a fresh crispness and confidence to the double-decker, with large windows, well-balanced deck proportions and attention to detail. Arguably it was the final and most complete implementation of the "square-box" design.

ECW's Titan-derived body: suffering from styling compromises? London was a major user.

The ECW body was later manufactured by Leyland Bus at Workington. There were detail changes, but the body was still recognisably related to the Titan. This is a Badgerline bus in Bath. Production of the Leyland body ceased in 1992.

developing a droop-fronted double-decker style with deep, multiple-curved coach-like windscreen. The effect was by no means universally liked, but some customers such as Leicester City Transport made it their standard body. East Lancs also offered an Alexander R-type body lookalike, with some versions looking more alike than others. Thus it arrived in the 1990s in the odd position of offering a basic double-decker that was actually modelled on someone else's design.

Among single-deckers, the field in 1980 was more limited. The basic choice was a Leyland National, whose Mk II version (just launched) took a lunge backwards in style by resuscitating a curved windscreen similar to the BET design of the 1960s. If you wanted a separate chassis, the standard choice was the straight-sided Duple Dominant bus.

There were, however, more exotic options such as the idiosyncratic Marshall Camair 80 and the then-new Plaxton Bustler, but neither sold in great numbers. If pressed, East Lancs could even offer you a body derived from the 20-year-old BET design. However, hard times were to prompt a new flowering in bus styling, and in the post-deregulation era the single-decker proved to be more attractive than the double-decker. It was therefore first to see the benefits.

Why did this happen? The simple answer is that the upheavals of the 1980s (deregulation, sale of national companies) reduced the giant bus groupings to smaller, more approachable operating units. These organisations were free from the buying traditions of their forebears, and at last they were willing to look at new bus designs without expecting to buy them in hundreds.

Even more encouraging for the makers, these operators did not insist rigidly on compatibility with existing body styles. They were now more interested in availability, first cost and whole-life operating cost.

Leyland was ahead of the game in meeting this new demand, launching its National single-decker replacement, the Lynx, in the late-1980s. With its upright profile and polygonal front face, complete with tilted driver's windscreen, it owed remarkably little to any other style of the time (although it has since proved the inspiration for the similar-looking Willowbrook Warrior). The Lynx was crisp, distinctive and different. Production endured into 1992, but history will probably position it as a bus of the 1980s, breaking the mould.

Otherwise, double-decker design plodded on unexcitingly through the 1980s. MCW managed to persuade most of its customers to accept a Mk II version of the Metrobus — rationalised in construction techniques, and visually not unlike the Alexander R-type. London however demurred (problems of compatibility, of course). Leyland dropped the Titan but persevered with the Olympian body to the end.

In some ways East Lancs was the most adventurous double-decker manufacturer of the period — offering bonded glazing to anyone who would accept it, and

The Alexander R-type set new standards when it was launched. A Busways' Scania shows the crisp lines.

Optare's VW-based City Pacer, with its confident loping front, brought an even greater change, and set the scene for the full sized DAF-based Delta that followed. Meanwhile Alexander developed its PS body, basing it on the angular and less well-liked P-type. Duple launched a long-awaited replacement for

East Lancs has been one of the most adventurous double-deck builders, offering bonded glazing and curved upper deck windscreens. A London & Country Volvo Citybus demonstrates the East Lancs look.

the Dominant bus, although its takeover by Plaxton soon put an end to that. However, East Lancs somehow managed to capture the essence of its frontal styling in its own new EL2000, so in spirit it lives on. The only problem with the EL2000 is that it has appeared in so many variants of screen, scuttle and rear end that it can be hard to recall just what the basic styling is supposed to be.

In the age of the minibus, the Dennis Dart rear-engined model rapidly became a benchmark for the industry and spawned a host of new body styles. The original Duple body, with its distinctive barrel windscreen and flared scuttle, could well turn out to be the most memorable example, but other striking designs have come from Wrights, Wadham Stringer and Reeve Burgess (now made by Plaxton). Alexander, East Lancs and Northern Counties have also produced Dart bodies, although with perhaps less radical styling.

The crisply-styled Leyland Lynx set new standards, and influenced Willowbrook's Warrior body. Hants & Sussex was an early Lynx user, albeit only for a short time.

The square-profile Reeve Burgess implementation, with distinctly continental overtones, might well have provided the basis for a full-sized single-decker — were it not for the fact that Plaxton itself already had its even more advanced, even more continentally-influenced Verde on the stocks. This was launched to wide acclaim in 1991.

What is ironical is that even as recently as 1980, fleet engineers would have been wringing their hands in horror at the thought of all this variety. Think of the extra cost of stocking two or three incompatible sizes of side window! Think of stocking even one large single-piece windscreen! Think of the special plastic mouldings for the front and rear domes, coverings and skirt panels!

Now engineers are willing to entertain all manner of newcomers. During the 1980s, some experimented with bus bodies by Van Hool and Neoplan; and since the turn of the 1990s several have been wooed by the straightforward but striking Ikarus-bodied DAF. What price compatibility now?

Among double-deckers, the star turn of the early-1990s is the Optare Spectra. Yet it is worth considering what the real changes in the Spectra are. The windows are deep, but not exceptional; and they are round-cornered — apparently a retrospective move in relation to the recent obsession with the direct-

The first body for the Dennis Dart, the Duple Dartline, had controversial styling with its curved front end. Now built by Marshall of Cambridge, it still looks good with its deep glazing and neat proportions.

glazed look. The windscreen is deep, but then so is the one on Alexander's R-type (in variants such as the one on Leyland Lion, at least). The back end is also reminiscent of the R-type's. So what's new?

It is in the detail that the Spectra scores. The front screens are round-cornered and made in a single piece

Round or square?

People who want to rail against buses (and there are always plenty of them) tend to complain about their so-called boxy designs. Yet until the new generation of buses came along, arguably the greatest step forward in bus design was the very move to boxiness.

Admittedly, if you like rounded styles no amount of rationalisation will convince you of the virtues of this. Bus writers and journalists still lament the passing of what they term the well-rounded style used in the heyday of bus design (effectively the 1930s and 1950s). To them, bus styling took an irredeemable lunge for the worse when the latter-day boxy designs came in.

Yet the change from rounded to square is in fact fundamental in the story of the bus. It marks the first enduring development in style (as opposed to

design) since the 1920s. Admittedly there was a blip during the War, when austerely angular utility bodies marked a sharp contrast with the curvaceous bodies of the 1930s. Yet curving designs reappeared soon afterwards and continued well into the 1960s.

Historians may cite the launch of the rear-engined double-decker or the underfloor-engined single-decker as turning points, but visually these buses inherited the style of their times. In the 1960s MCW, Park Royal and Roe discovered angular corners, and buses never looked the same again.

Like it or not, bus designs have been boxy for as long now as they were rounded before, and seem unlikely to revert in the foreseeable future. And the extra internal space and bigger windows have brought far brighter, airier interiors. What the 1990s have bestowed is a new sense of flair — an attention to detail and a curved-edged look that give a softness to the square design.

The Reeve Burgess Pointer, now built by Plaxton, has a square profile with continental overtones. The first customer for a Pointer was Southampton Citybus.

(and hang the cost). The moulded side skirts have a subtly curved lower edge, and so do the matching bumpers. The front grille is discreet and car-like, not overblown and botched as in so many bus designs. There is no peak to the front dome, yet it's not curved either. In fact it's not what you'll call a 'dome' at all — just a simple strip. But then who said there had to be a dome, anyway?

Above all, the Spectra's design hangs together. It's all of a piece. It looks as though it was designed by one person, not a committee. Hard to define, but clear enough in the execution. It tells customers that bus styles have moved forward. As I write, a revised double-decker from Northern Counties is awaited. The new generation is reaching maturity at last.

Does this all matter? To the enthusiast, perhaps not. I personally don't look forward with any enthusiasm to a world bereft of Routemasters, for all their small windows and rounded domes. But styling in buses should be about more than just nostalgia. Buses can only have an existence in so far as they offer an attractive means of travel. That is bound up in a lot of things — their accessibility, their internal design, their speed and the nature of the service they run. But it's also influenced by what buses look like: perhaps more than we think.

Below:
The Optare Spectra brings new style to double-deckers.

OLD BUSES NEVER DIE . . . THEY SIMPLY GET REFURBISHED!

Stephen Morris considers the growing trend to have old buses refurbished, and concludes that it's not such a new idea

One of the more fascinating aspects of the bus industry, and one which has probably done much to retain or stimulate the interest of many an enthusiast, is its ingenuity. Major operators have long known just what they want to operate their particular services. The fact that it wasn't available in any manufacturers' catalogue was academic; they would get it built somewhere. Even then they wouldn't leave it alone for very long before introducing their own modifications.

But even greater ingenuity than developing individual operator specifications or introducing modifications has been shown down the years by operators wanting to get a little more life out of a bus. This has been done in a number of ways, ranging from minor cosmetic titivation to rebuilding on a scale

redolent of the proverbial 15-year-old hammer with a new head and a new handle. This could be undertaken in the operator's own central works, or it could be done by or in conjunction with a body manufacturer. These days precious few operators have the impressive central works facilities which once turned out such masterpieces, but more than one bodybuilder has cause to be thankful in these straitened times that it was able to offer refurbishing or rebodying, and at least one, Willowbrook, survives almost entirely on rebodying old chassis.

A Beadle/Leyland rebuild, formerly in the Maidstone & District fleet, seen with Thornes, Bubwith, in 1970.
MICHAEL FOWLER

Eastern Counties A226 (VG 4824) was a Leyland Titan TD2, refurbished and rebodied after the war with a new ECW lowbridge body.

And it is straitened times which usually create a demand for refurbishing in its many forms. These days it is big business, and that's because so few operators have the cash to buy the new buses to create the impression they would like to. Other periods of refurbishing have often been in times of adversity too, and prior to the present era probably the war years did more to further the cause of refurbishing than any other.

There were various reasons for this. The main one was that after the war there simply wasn't the capacity to build new buses (or new anything, really) in the quantities which were required. Production could only build up slowly as workers were demobbed, factory premises were rebuilt after sustaining bomb damage or were simply worn out from years of massive war production and little time to stop and maintain machinery. Then, much of what was produced had to be exported to give the country the chance to get back on an even keel economically.

Meanwhile bus operators were desperate for new rolling stock. Fleet replacement programmes had come to an untimely halt and even comparatively recent prewar vehicles had aged prematurely due to sheer hard work and enforced neglect.

The war also sowed the seeds for another bout of rebuilding, by introducing the utility bus. This involved very rugged, basic chassis by Guy or Daimler (Bedford in the case of single-deckers) with bodywork built to an uncomfortably basic standard from whatever materials were available — not always the best! It took only a few years for the sub-standard bodies to be shaken to pieces by rigidly-mounted Gardner 5LW engines in chassis which could probably go on for ever — an ideal combination for refurbishing or rebodying.

Creations resulting from the mania for refurbishing, rebuilding and rebodying in those early postwar years were many and varied. Possibly the most extreme examples were those produced by Beadle of Dartford, in which prewar components from Leylands and AECs (in the main) were put together in a new integral construction. It mattered not whether the components came from single-deckers or double-deckers, as many were common to both anyway in the half-cab era, and the resulting vehicle was a stylish, full-fronted coach which to the average passenger in the late-1940s/early-1950s was perfectly acceptable as a modern vehicle. Leyland in particular enjoyed a reputation for the very refined nature of its prewar product, so there was no problem on that front.

Beadle also built service buses in the same way, often using parts from Bedfords, though other types were also used with varying results. They found their way into a number of major fleets, the Leyland and AEC-based ones featuring mainly in BET fleets on the south coast, with Tilling companies such as Eastern Counties being the main customers for Bedfords, and other things such as Dennisses and Leyland Cubs, mainly for rural work. Later Beadle used its experience of integral construction to build its own new integrals, often using the very compact and innovative Commer TS3 two-stroke engine, though with the usual bus operator preference for six big pots with conventional valve gear and avoiding complexities such as superchargers and horizontally-opposed pistons, they met with limited success.

Many of the Tilling Group companies practised major rebuilding of prewar buses. By the late-1930s most had settled on the Bristol/ECW standard, more often than not with Gardner 5LW engines for the ultimate in economy. Many still had non-standard buses from the early-1930s or even late-1920s at the end of the war, often Leylands, and it was commonplace to bring in standardisation by installing Gardner 5LWs in place of well-worn Leyland units and either remodelling the body to modern standards or taking it off altogether and replacing it with the current standard ECW product. More often than not

Above and below:
London wartime Daimler CWA6 D51 (GXV 782) is seen at Clapham and then sometime later, following rebodying by Harkness, in Belfast in 1963.
F. G. REYNOLDS/R. M. LEE

the effect was completed by replacing the radiator with a more modern Covrad design by Coventry Radiators and approved by Leyland, producing a bus which bore no resemblance to its origins as a TD2 or whatever, and was really a sort of home-made Bristol K5G in all but name.

During the 1950s attention turned to sorting out the problems of wartime utilities. Some of the larger operators simply got rid of them as soon as possible. Procurement of new buses during the war was often a case of Hobson's choice, and if Guy Arabs or Daimler CWA6s didn't fit your ideas on standardisation, then tough! In some cases this actually led to the operator changing allegiance to the manufacturer concerned, particularly in the case of Guy, which was little-known before the war but soon showed itself able to produce a product which was rugged, indestructible and economical, if a little short on frills. But often wartime products, with basic bodywork which soon showed itself in need of attention, with unseasoned timbers rotting away, were often replaced as soon as new deliveries allowed. This brought floods of serviceable chassis on to the market, and London Guys and Daimlers in particular turned up in various

Typical of more gentle refurbishing of utility buses is this 1945 Strachan-bodied Guy Arab II of Barton. With more modern window styling it makes quite a smart-looking bus.

aces, very often in quite a new 'guise' (sorry!). Both elfast and Edinburgh swallowed their pride and ought London cast-offs, though in both cases with rand new bodywork which in the case of Belfast lended in imperceptibly with 'real' new buses, even the lack of 'Z's or 'I's in their registrations gave the ame away.

Belfast took no less than 100 ex-London Daimler WA6s in 1953/54. They entered service with just a ttle cosmetic tidying up, but were all rebodied in 955/56 by Harkness, which had earlier rebodied 42 f Belfast's own CWA6s using Metsec frames. The nassis were also improved with the fitting of flexible ngine mountings. The London vehicles were to put in nother 15 years' service for Belfast so most had roved a very good buy. Some survived long enough be destroyed in the 'Troubles'.

Meanwhile Edinburgh relieved London of 60 Guy rabs and had them rebodied by Duple, most of them the Nudd Bros & Lockyer factory, which was later become Duple (Midland), in 1952/53. Edinburgh's x-London Guys were given very distinctive, and nodern, new bodies, with quasi full-fronts, concealed diators and four-bay construction. So thorough was e rebuilding that new chassis numbers were issued, nabling them to be re-registered JWS 581-640. None ut the *cognoscenti* would guess that these stylish-oking buses with Edinburgh registrations originated wartime London. They lasted into the 1960s, and ere really something of a bargain; Edinburgh had id only £60 per chassis, though the bodies added ther more to the price — £1,725 a time!

Edinburgh also had some of its own CWG5s bodied by Alexander in 1954, and another 60 ondon Guys came north, 23 rebuilt as single-deckers r Highland and Scottish Omnibuses and 37 going to estern SMT, all rebodied, mostly by Alexander or

Northern Counties, but eight received postwar Croft bodies which had themselves adorned prewar chassis.

Other London wartime cast-offs saw service elsewhere, many going to Ceylon, though several of the Guys went to Rhodesia where they too were rebodied as single-deckers.

London had also had 29 wartime Bristol Ks and it was hardly surprising that many of these quickly went off to Tilling companies, who were a little more attuned to the qualities of the type than London, and many of them were rebodied by ECW for Crosville, though only after receiving late-wartime bodies taken off prewar chassis. Four were also rebodied for Brighton Hove & District in the mid-1950s.

Other operators had their own wartime stock rebodied; Maidstone & District for one had 100 wartime Bristol K6As, some of which had had secondhand bodies when new, rebodied with attractive Weymann bodies in the 1950s, and North Western had wartime Guys and late prewar Bristol K5Gs less successfully rebodied by Willowbrook, unusually retaining the original prewar high-mounted radiators on its Bristols. Many of the Tilling companies had the postwar PV2 radiator fitted on their postwar rebodies, such that it took great powers of observation to distinguish them from the genuine postwar article.

Despite their shortcomings, however, not all utilities were rebodied or consigned to the scrapyard, and several operators instead gave them more gentle refurbishing, some to very good effect, for the basic outline of the utility body was quite pleasing and with

31

North Western had both wartime Guy Arabs and prewar Bristols rebodied by Willowbrook. Examples of both are visible here in Manchester Piccadilly in 1952.
G. H. F. ATKINS

more modern detailing such as rounded window pans they could be made to look quite attractive — though inevitably some operators fell wide of the mark when modernising their bodies!

The standard wartime single-decker was the Bedford OWB, which was essentially very similar to the peacetime OB, and again substandard bus bodies had been fitted. Not surprisingly a good number were rebodied after the war with standard postwar coach bodies and were difficult to tell apart from new OBs.

Large-scale refurbishing seems to go in cycles, and is usually affected by some external influence. Thus the next phase of refurbishing came about in the late-1950s/early-1960s and was due to the fact that underfloor-engined single-deckers had rendered the half-cab type obsolete almost overnight. Again the war can be seen as having some influence here; just before the war underfloor-engined designs were just beginning to emerge, and no doubt had development not been curtailed in 1939 they would have come to fruition somewhat earlier. As it was, postwar production resumed with updated versions of prewar half-cab designs, and these sold well as operators were

short of new rolling stock. However, when underfloor-engined vehicle production began in earnest from 1949 half-cab single-deckers quickly began to appear old-fashioned. Not only that, as one-man operation came in, then the underfloor-engined designs, which could carry at least five more passengers than a comparable half-cab single-decker, if not more, appeared yet more attractive. The problem was that chassis like the Leyland Tiger PS1 and PS2 were built to last and it was difficult to justify scrapping very serviceable vehicles just because they were old-fashioned. Some rear-entrance vehicles were converted to forward entrance, to facilitate one-man operation, and in some cases half-cabs were rebuilt to full-front.

But another solution was to rebuild them as double-deckers. There was not a great deal of difference between a Leyland Titan and a Leyland Tiger, and thus certain operators set about a rebuilding programme with gusto. Prominent was the Ulster Transport Authority, which had a lot of postwar Tiger and had 158 rebuilt with MCW-framed bodywork as rear-entrance double-deckers. The concept was popular in Yorkshire too. Yorkshire Woollen set the ball rolling, by rebodying 24 PS1s with Metro-Cammell double-deck bodywork in 1954/55. Yorkshire Traction had 27 PS1s rebuilt as rear-entrance double-deckers by Roe in 1956/57, followed

y nine PS2s with forward-entrance double-deck
bodywork by Roe and Northern Counties in 1960/61.
Both operators then had Yorkshire Woollen PS2
chassis rebodied as forward-entrance double-deckers
in 1963, nine with Northern Counties bodywork for
Yorkshire Traction and six with Roe for Woollen.
West Riding too had nine PS1s bodied as double-
deckers by Roe in 1956, while in Huddersfield, lest it
be thought that all such activities were confined to
Leylands, Hansons put together seven of its own AEC
Regents from AEC Regal bits, having them bodied by

Roe, and also built up eight single-deckers, also from
Regal bits, and had those bodied with full-front
bodywork, capable of one-man operation, by Roe.
They were unusual amongst Regals in having Regent
V-style radiator grilles, which gave them a very

Hanson, the Huddersfield independent, was quite innovative
with its use of old AEC parts, resulting in this forward-entrance
Regent III and full-front Regals with Regent V-style grilles. All
had been rebodied by Roe in the 1960s.
MICHAEL FOWLER

distinctive appearance, although the double-deckers retained traditional AEC-style exposed radiators, something of an anachronism when the last was built in 1963, and looking quite unusual on forward-entrance buses. They used parts from 7ft 6in wide vehicles rebuilt to 8ft.

Barton was another independent which undertook a good deal of refurbishing, and it too rebuilt Tigers as double-deckers, amassing a fleet of more than 20 and fitting O.600 engines in vehicles which had originated as PS1s to give the requisite power output for a double-decker. Meanwhile other operators used parts of Tigers in rebuilds; CIE for one used Tiger parts, though with new PD3 frames, to build its last half-cabs, the R900-series, which had St Helens-style bonnets.

Such extreme means to prolong the active life of buses began to die out during the 1960s. The seven-year overhaul cycle practised by major operators to fit in with the seven-year Certificate of Fitness system which used to govern the roadworthiness of buses did give the opportunity to tinker with buses, and quite often vehicles would emerge from their first major overhaul with detail differences, and maybe some rebuilding where the original construction of the bus

was a bit suspect. But with the upheavals of war behind the industry, buses built from the mid-1950s onwards were generally pretty robust and all the mainstream manufacturers had quite serviceable underfloor-engined single-deckers on the market.

Then from 1968, when operators were beginning to wonder what to do with half-cab double-deckers now that one-man operation was legal on all types of suitably-equipped buses, government grants were introduced to buy new vehicles capable for one-man operation and meeting set specifications. Grants were fixed at 25% and then increased to 50%, so it was cheaper and more effective to buy new, even if it meant discarding buses which were mechanically and structurally well up to several years' further service. For smaller operators in particular a new breed of single-decker grew up, based on lightweight Bedford or Ford chassis with bodywork by concerns such as Willowbrook and Duple, which were cheap and cheerful, attracted bus grant and, at a push, could carry as many people as a double-decker, all without needing a conductor. This was not only a more effective expedient than making do and mending with old stock, it was also cheaper and the refurbishing business became a rarity. National Bus Company looked at the possibility of refurbishing to extend service life when Bus Grant came under threat with the election of Margaret Thatcher's government in 1979, and a Yorkshire Traction Leyland Leopard service bus was heavily modified and brought up to

With Leyland Lynx-style squareness, RFC 14T is a Willowbrook Warrior-rebodied Leyland Leopard of Oxford Bus Co, seen at the 1991 Southampton Coach Rally. It was new with Duple bodywork as a Citylink coach for the London service.
STEPHEN MORRIS

he standards of the day. It remained a one-off, and most fleets had a young age profile anyway. If Leyland Nationals weren't everyone's cup of tea, they were at least modern and youthful.

Thus with a few isolated exceptions the present era is the first for some time to return to the concept of major refurbishing. The foregoing shows that the concept is far from new, and the present refurbishing mania has a number of parallels with previous eras. It also has the important difference that operators have tended to abandon their engineering skills from earlier days, for a number of reasons, so refurbishing is usually done by outside specialists and tends to follow more standardised patterns as a result.

The desire to extend the life of buses again is due to a number of factors. Obviously the end of New Bus Grant, coming at a time when passenger revenue was in sharp decline, had a direct effect. Buses were just too expensive for many to buy. Coupled with that was the uncertainty of deregulation, and in many cases the money which might be used for fleet replacement was tied up in seeing off competition. Then many major companies have been privatised, and money which could have been used for new rolling stock is being used to capitalise the company, pay off capital debts or to buy up other companies newly on the market.

Then there is the effect of Bus Grant itself; a nice new fleet of buses bought to see off half-cabs and extend one-man operation in 1975 was nicely ripe at the time of deregulation and is now an ageing

embarrassment, too expensive now to replace *en masse* but looking decidedly tired.

There are basically three strands to the current refurbishing mania. There is the approach of taking a good solid old bus, stripping out some of its worn bits, titivating the interior, bringing certain aspects up to modern standards and generally sprucing up. This is the approach taken by London Buses to keep its Routemasters on the road and by Cheltenham & Gloucester's 'National 3' project. Then there is straightforward rebodying, giving all the appearance of a new bus for half the price, albeit with the bits under the floor still making lots of noise and feeling the bumps in roads which too need refurbishing. Or there is the complete renewing of existing vehicles, of which the principal exponent is East Lancs with its ambitious National Greenway project. Bring your old Leyland National in at one end and come back a few weeks later to drive home in a nice, shiny 'new' bus.

Rebodying has helped at least three bodybuilders survive the famine of new orders. Willowbrook's Warrior body is available almost exclusively on old chassis, although one new ACE Puma has received that body. It's a basic, functional body, not especially pretty and owing more than a little in style to the

Also rebodied is this Leyland Leopard. The chassis was originally Shamrock & Rambler 3021 (REL 401R) and it was rebodied for Compass Bus, Wakefield, by Plaxton in 1987 as KIB 6110.
J. K. GRIME

East Lancs has been very busy rebodying chassis. This Leyland Tiger is one of 40 on ex-London Country chassis for Midland Red North. No 1723 (B103 KPF) originally had a high-floor Berkhof body.
ADRIAN PEARSON

quantities for coach work up to the early-1980s. As a coach chassis it has passed its prime; steel suspension and the lack of rear shock absorbers give it a rough ride compared with today's air-sprung sophisticates. It creates a fearful din, loved only by those who revel in good old Leyland sound effects (including the author!) and has over-long gearing to give it a high top speed, so it dies on long hills. Not only that but NBC in its infinite wisdom endowed its newest ones with dual-purpose bodywork lacking, shall we say, some of the enduring qualities of the chassis (even when new one type leaked like a sieve while the other had an embarrassing lack of integrity at the back end) so it is no hardship to consign the superstructure to the scrapyard and put a new bus body on. The other shortcomings of the chassis are only really of concern to coach operators; the fact that it won't romp along all day at 70mph regardless is of little consequence when trundling around the lanes of Sussex, and the noise and bounce has only to be endured by passengers for minutes rather than hours at a time.

City of Oxford is the only large operator to have taken to the Warrior to any extent, having a ready supply of old Leopards which have been supplanted by a new generation of coaches on the London service. That an operator deems the Leopard worthy of such treatment after ten years' hard labour thrashing up and down the M40 between Oxford and London, taking an advertised 100min, umpteen times a day is no little testimony to its dependability.

East Lancs has made quite a business of rebodying. Unkindly, it could be said that in recent years East Lancs had taken a 'mix-&-match' approach to bodybuilding, putting together virtually anything from the parts bin to suit the individual operator. However, its EL2000 single-deck body has a rather more cohesive appearance and forms the basis of a good rebodying package, as well as being available for new chassis. As a new vehicle, it has appeared on Dennis Falcon chassis for Drawlane (now British Bus) companies and Leicester CityBus, and on Volvo B10M for operators such as Blackburn and Northampton. It also adorns older chassis, including the Leyland Leopard, Tiger and older Volvos.

The Tiger is probably the most numerous chassis to be rebodied by East Lancs, and again there is a specific reason for this. Midland Red North, like East Lancs a subsidiary of British Bus, needed more high-capacity single-deck buses; meanwhile fellow British Bus subsidiary (though it was Drawlane at the time) London & Country had surplus Tigers from Green Line work. The first were 11m vehicles with ECW bodywork, and these were quickly stripped and

Amongst the most extreme examples of rebuilding recently was when Grey-Green had a batch of 12m Volvo B10M coaches rebodied as double-deckers by East Lancs. 164 (B864 XYR) looks like the purpose-built Volvo Citybuses in the fleet until one notices the position of the rear axle to accommodate the 6.1m wheelbase!
N. COLEMAN

standard independents' bus body until recently, the Duple Dominant, though with strong overtones of Leyland Lynx about it. It goes best on mid-engined chassis, and by far the most popular chassis to go under it is the faithful old Leopard, though the Bedford YMT or Leyland Tiger does just as well.

The Leopard is ideal though. It is a chassis built in the old Leyland tradition, ie solid as a rock, and in most instances it was built with semi-automatic transmission and is thus good for bus work, even if the high steps are a problem. It was built in huge

Grey-Green also has B10Ms rebodied as single-deckers by East Lancs. The length of the wheelbase is less noticeable on these than on the double-deckers.
M. KING

rebodied for MRN. Later ones are perhaps a little more controversial, being some four years newer and having much more solid and highly-specified 12m Berkhof high-floor bodies. But they were surplus to requirements and due to the depressed state of the coach market at the time and high stocks of secondhand coaches at the dealers their market value was somewhat diminished. So off came the Berkhofs and on went more EL2000s. Around 40 Tigers have been involved in the exercise, and they have provided Midland Red North with a useful fleet of stylish, modern, high-capacity single-deckers with air suspension and able to cruise at a good speed when required.

A particularly interesting spin-off of the EL2000 is the Atlantean Sprint, whereby the same single-deck body is used on old Atlantean double-decker chassis, reversing the old trend of rebodying PS-model Tigers as double-deckers! The first one was based on a short-wheelbase

HTR 568P is an East Lancs Atlantean Sprint, based on the chassis of a Southampton Citybus double-decker. It is seen in service with Brighton Borough Transport, though still owned by Southampton Citybus.
C. D. JONES

Southampton chassis, and gave the impression that the Sprint would be a good alternative to the Dennis Dart in the midibus sector. Quite who would want a midibus of such weight, pushed along by over 11 litres of solidly-built diesel engine (nearly twice as big as the Dart's engine!) was perhaps questionable, but in fact it made a remarkably good midibus. Being a full 2.5m wide it was much more spacious than a Dart, and being on a rear-engined double-deck chassis boasted a very good entrance. When we looked at the prototype at Coach & Bus we wondered rather who could want such a thing, but were soon won over to it. But perhaps our initial thought was right, as not many have been built. Southampton ordered 10, but a 35-seater weighing in at nearly eight and a half tons unladen has to be a bit of an extravagance! In the end Southampton reduced its order to five.

However, that is not the end of that particular story, as Sheffield Omnibus and Catch-A-Bus have had a couple built, not as super-heavyweight Darts but, with the chassis being lengthened, as very acceptable 47-seater single-deckers, which begins to make more sense.

While the Atlantean Sprint concept reversed the old trend for rebodying single-deckers as double-deckers, practised in the 1960s, Grey-Green recently reverted to that idea. As underfloor-engined single-deckers became the norm the opportunity to rebody single-deckers as double-deckers virtually disappeared. However, Volvo's Citybus double-decker was based fairly and squarely on the B10M coach chassis, and when Grey-Green needed more double-deckers for London contract services and had some middle-aged B10M coaches surplus to requirements, there was only one logical thing to do. Like Midland Red North's Tigers, these Volvos' values were depressed by the state of the coach market, so off came the Plaxton Paramount coach bodies, and on went new East Lancs double-deck bodies. The only thing was they were 12m coaches, on the standard Volvo 6.1m wheelbase, about a metre longer than the standard Citybus wheelbase, but no matter; they just came out with the back wheels a bit nearer the back than usual! They looked a bit strange, but fulfilled a purpose. Low-profile tyres brought the frame height down a bit. They remain unique as single-deck underfloor-engined coaches rebuilt to double-deck, and some single-deckers were built in the same way at the same time.

A Leyland National being prepared for the Greenway treatment at East Lancs. Note how the vehicle has been stripped right down to its bare frame and looks like an elaborate Meccano set at this stage!
STEPHEN MORRIS

The prototype National Greenway, London & Country 252, at Weybridge. The original bus was new to Ribble and came from North Western.
STEPHEN MORRIS

Northern Counties too has been thankful for refurbishing and rebodying work to get it through the stickiest patch in its history. Indeed in one of the comparatively rare examples of rebodying in the early-1980s, it rebodied some Fleetlines for Southend, whilst later on in the decade it rebodied some very elderly Atlanteans for Cleveland. It has been doing rather more recently. Of particular interest is some of the work it has been doing for Fylde Borough Transport, involving major refurbishing of some of its Atlanteans, complete with new front and rear ends, and, in some cases, even moving the radiator out of the engine compartment up to the front end. The next stage is the rebodying of some ex-Hull long-wheelbase Atlanteans for Fylde with single-deck Paladin bodies.

The London Routemaster and National Greenway approach both have one thing in common: they involve the use of a good solid structure which is still very serviceable but needs attention to points of detail and mechanical components.

The Routemaster story is remarkable by any stretch of the imagination. To suggest in these august columns that the Routemaster shouldn't be allowed to continue in regular London service until its centenary or beyond is probably even more likely to provoke an earbashing for the writer than did his disparaging remarks about North Western's Bristol L5Gs last year, so he will refrain. But it must say something about the lack of investment in research and development in Britain that the most successful bus in the capital was designed nearly 40 years ago, about the same time as that other icon of London's transport, the FX4 taxi. Like the FX4 it looks set to be with us until the end of time, or at least until the end of the decade.

Purists no doubt would prefer Routemasters to have been left alone. There is something rather soulless about the undistinguished burble of a Cummins engine, whether it be an L10, B-series or the C-series now powering just over half the remaining Routemaster fleet. Worse is the thought that something *Italian* could be powering the other examples of that symbol of the Great British Empire. It is not as satisfying as the sound of an AEC AV590, or even a Leyland O.600. But at least it has enabled the Routemaster to continue in service, while the old AECs get to the stage where they simply cannot be overhauled again and spares get ever more scarce. They also put out less nasty stuff into the atmosphere, with more recent developments in combustion, injection and induction technology.

And internally the Routemaster, though a paragon of 1950s design, was getting a bit past it. Open tungsten bulbs may evoke happy memories but aren't as good as modern fluorescent lights when it comes to dispelling the darkness. Compared with most modern buses Routemasters have small windows and a basically dark interior which was beginning to look dingy. Whether one likes the new look or not, with its cheerful moquette, lower-deck soft trim, brighter colours and new lighting, the refurbished Routemaster is certainly lighter inside, and has more the air of a conveyance of the 1990s.

The rest of the Routemaster refurbishing has been to eliminate obsolete parts and to minimise damage; metal domes have been replaced by a plastic compound which springs back to shape after the inevitable encounters with trees, for instance, and external lighting too is now up to 1990s standards. *Both* headlights work on dipped beam now, which must be very radical, and there are two stoplights and new-fangled direction indicators at the back.

The refurbishing on this scale of buses aged between 25 and 30 years old is certainly unprecedented. The cost has been about £22,000 per bus — not including the new engine!

The East Lancs approach to refurbishing Leyland Nationals is yet more expensive and also more extensive. Unlike the Routemaster, which comes out of the mill still looking very much like a Routemaster, the National Greenway emerges virtually as a new bus built around the very solid frame of an old Leyland National. Say what you like about the Leyland National, but Leyland's structural engineers in the late-1960s certainly got their sums right, and whilst they went for steel rather than the Routemaster's aluminium they also got their corrosion treatment programme pretty well right, bar a few bits round the wheelarches which tend to give up the ghost before the rest.

The fixed-head Leyland 500-series engine was less well thought-out, and some of the interior fittings were rather below par, so the fact that Leyland Nationals sound very often to be rattling from all ends at once is not in fact down to any structural weakness as it might be on other buses. Basically the National Greenway

project takes in an old National, strips its right down to the bare frame — though the roof stays put — and uses that as the basis for a new bus. The operator can bring in an old National for treatment, or East Lancs can find a 'donor' bus, usually through its fellow British Bus subsidiaries, North Western being a particular favourite. The structure is reclad in aluminium, with the option of a grp skirt and the stress panels are put inside rather than outside. This means if you then bend a panel in service it can be replaced by any old piece of tin which will fit, rather than a properly stressed piece. And that is increasingly the way cash-starved bus operators have to work these days. New front and rear ends are fitted, the interior is retrimmed and anything mechanical which can wear is replaced. When conceived only the Gardner 6HLXB engine was fitted, either new or reconditioned either by Gardner itself or by Paul Gardner Engineering. However, rumours surrounding the future of Gardner have led operators to panic into requiring other makes of engine (it is noteworthy how often rumours can become self-fulfilling prophecies in this way), so when London General decided to have its Red Arrow fleet 'Greenway-ised' and specified DAF engines, East Lancs was scarcely in a position to quibble. Since then Blackburn Transport has specified Volvo engines in its batch of eight.

The original styling of the prototype was not universally acclaimed; the project had originated with London & Country and that company's livery helped the looks of the first one to an extent, but it was still no oil painting, so London General asked Ray Stenning to tidy up its looks, and the revised style has also been specified by London & Country for its first production batch. Others so far, all of the 'old' style, have gone to C-Line, SUT, Kentish Bus and East Yorkshire.

The resulting vehicle lacks the cohesive styling of the original Leyland National, but gives all the appearance of a new bus and lacks all the bangs and rattles of that vehicle. The ride quality is superb and even the sound of the Gardner 6HLXB seems muted; it is certainly a passenger-friendly bus and incorporates most of the features of DiPTAC to aid less mobile and partially-sighted passengers. East Lancs reckons on a 10-year life.

Maybe the bus industry will eventually get back to being able to buy lots of new buses again. It certainly needs to address the problem of its ageing vehicle fleet quite soon, and pressures to clean up the environment will doubtless mean that ancient bus engines will have to be renewed with something cleaner before long. In the meantime refurbishing will no doubt continue to be popular. At least many of the public will be fooled into thinking they're riding on new buses — even if some of us know better!

FLASHBACK: 20 YEARS AGO

In 1974 Britain's bus industry was in the throes of change. **Stewart J. Brown** looks back.

It's 1974. Mark III Cortinas are the order of the day unless you're keen on ugly cars in which case you might fancy one of the recently-introduced Austin Allegros. Austin have made history by re-inventing the wheel and the steering wheel is not round — no kidding! — it's quartic, which means it's shaped vaguely like a TV screen. Dissatisfied owners complained and Austin offer round replacements.

The bus industry is in the throes of change. Again. This time it's a direct result of local government reorganisation in England and Wales. Scotland has to wait another 12 months for its local government to be restructured. Metropolitan counties appear in the four English conurbations which already have Passenger Transport Executives and in two new areas — West Yorkshire and South Yorkshire. A number of authorities get trendy new names like Thamesdown, which sounds as if it should be in Essex but turns out, rather surprisingly, to be in Wiltshire.

Urban district councils vanish and new, bigger, district councils take their place. This leads to a number of municipal mergers. Names like Bedwas & Machen will cease to trip off bus enthusiasts' tongues. The tiny South Wales municipal bus fleet has been united with two of its neighbours in the new Rhymney Valley operation.

The National Bus Company is at its peak, employing an amazing 69,574 people and operating 20,469 buses and coaches. This is the last year in which NBC's vehicle fleet tops the 20,000 mark. The Scottish Bus Group is running 4,514 vehicles, a figure which falls gradually as the decade moves on.

Bradford's municipal buses were absorbed by the newly-created West Yorkshire PTE in 1974. Typical of the older vehicles in the fleet is this 1963 Metro-Cammell-bodied AEC Regent V.
ALL PHOTOS BY STEWART J. BROWN.

Top:
Huddersfield's bright red and cream livery was replaced by West Yorkshire PTE verona green and cream. A 1963 Roe-bodied PD3A basks in the March sunshine days before Huddersfield's absorption by the PTE.

Above:
Waveney was a new name in 1974, taking over the small Lowestoft Corporation operation. The fleet's newest buses were AEC Swifts with bodies built in the town by ECW.

NBC's corporate identity, with the imposition of poppy red or leaf green liveries to its subsidiary fleets throughout England and Wales is proceeding apace. New buses are delivered in the approved colours; old ones are gradually being repainted. Traditional liveries are disappearing and purists are grumbling.

New double-deck bus models are appearing prophetically — although nobody realises it at the time — with strong Swedish connections. Scottish-based Ailsa Bus reveal a new front-engined model which has been designed to counter SBG criticisms of the unreliability of new-fangled rear-engined buses, a breed which SBG's conservative engineers are unwilling or unable to come to terms with. To accommodate a front engine and a front entrance, the Ailsa uses a small turbocharged power unit, Volvo's 6.7-litre TD70E engine. This is the smallest engine ever fitted to a production British double-decker. By the end of the year four have been completed — a demonstrator in the livery of Alexander (Midland) and three for the West Midlands PTE. But there are plenty more to come.

SBG's distrust of rear engines is graphically illustrated by the conclusion in the spring of the

exchange with NBC of its fleet of almost 250 VRTs for a like number of trusty front-engined FLFs.

The other newcomer is the Metropolitan, an amalgam of Scania running units and MCW bodywork. A dual-door demonstrator is doing the rounds and deliveries to operators during the year see Metropolitans running for Leicester City Transport (eight), Merseyside PTE (20), Greater Manchester PTE (10) and the first of an order for 40 for Greater Glasgow PTE.

The Metropolitan has an 11-litre Scania engine which delivers outstanding performance at the expense of fuel economy. But the Metropolitan's weakness proves to be the steel-framed body which rots so badly that few of the breed are overhauled for further service when their initial seven year Certificates of Fitness expire. The Metropolitan follows another joint Scania-MCW project, the single-deck Metro-Scania, production of which came to the end in 1973.

Mainstream double-deck deliveries are of the three established models — Daimler Fleetline, Leyland Atlantean and Bristol VRT. The VRT with ECW body is the standard NBC double-decker but a number of VRTs, uniquely with MCW bodies, are delivered to the West Midlands PTE whose standard bus is the Fleetline. One reason for this is that there are major hiccups in Fleetline deliveries because of the large orders which have been placed by London Transport and by Leyland's decision to switch Fleetline

Many NBC buses still wore old liveries. A 1959 Atlantean with lowbridge Weymann bodywork pulls out of Doncaster's south bus station in Yorkshire Traction's bright red and cream.

Accrington became Hyndburn in 1974, but retained the striking dark blue and red livery of its predecessor. An East Lancs-bodied Guy Arab heads through the town centre.

production from Coventry to Lancashire which exacerbates the delays. By ordering VRTs West Midlands is at least able to standardise on Gardner-engined chassis.

London seems well-pleased with its new Fleetlines which are ousting ageing RTs and the unfortunate and unreliable single-deck Merlins. Initial Fleetline orders have totalled over 1,700, of which a good number are now in service. In 1974 an order is placed for a further 679, along with 164 of the new MCW Metropolitan. The year also sees the delivery of the first London Fleetlines designed for crew-operation and classed as DM, instead of DMS, the coding used for the original one-person-operated versions.

With double-deck opo still a relatively new phenomenon, a number of operators are undecided about the best way of speeding passenger flows. Cities such as Nottingham and Edinburgh are convinced that two-door buses are the answer, but elsewhere operators are less sure and some are now reverting to single-door buses.

Below:
A Hants & Dorset Bristol MW6G in Southampton retains Tilling colours but with corporate NBC style fleetname. Hants & Dorset's livery changed from green to red under NBC control.

Below:
Another fleet to undergo a change of colour was West Riding. Two Fleetlines in Leeds make the point. The lead vehicle has Northern Counties bodywork and wears West Riding's somewhat dull green. The Roe-bodied bus behind has been freshly repainted in poppy red.

Bottom:
East Kent was unusual in rebodying coaches in the early-1970s. This is a 1962 Reliance with a 1973 Plaxton body which pays lip service to the NBC edict on corporate livery, with white relief (instead of cream) and NBC lettering but no double-N logo.

45

The changes which come with local government reorganisation are far reaching. They take place on 1 April, which cynics might reckon to be an appropriate date. Twelve municipal fleets are renamed; three undertakings are enlarged; eight are absorbed by the two new PTEs; and four are taken over by three of the established PTEs whose boundaries are redrawn.

For the renamed municipal fleets there is little change other than new crests or fleetnames. Those involved in amalgamations opt for new liveries. The enlarged Blackburn fleet adopts a green, white and red colour scheme. Blackburn's buses had been green, Darwen's red. The new Lancaster City Transport fleet breaks with the traditions of its precursors, abandoning Lancaster's dark red and Morecambe's green for a totally new blue livery. Rhymney Valley, which combines three Welsh fleets — Caerphilly (green/cream), Rhymney Valley (patriotic red, white and green) and Bedwas & Machen (blue/cream) — adopts a smart new brown, yellow and cream. Cleveland Transit abandons Teesside's somewhat nondescript turquoise for a strong new green and yellow combination.

The PTE changes see new colours too. Merseyside is enlarged to take in two fleets which are red and cream, St Helens and Southport. The PTE already has two liveries — green in Liverpool and blue on the Wirral — and it decides to adopt a green scheme for its entire fleet, with a new Merseyside fleetname to replace the original PTE logo. In a nice touch the new fleetname is produced in red for buses in the two

newly-acquired fleets until such times as they are repainted green. The new livery demonstrates to the good citizens of genteel Southport that they now live in a suburb of Liverpool.

West Yorkshire toys with the idea of divisional liveries with a common layout based on cream (or buttermilk as the PTE describes it). The relief colours are based on the previous municipal colours — green in Leeds, red in Huddersfield, blue in Bradford and orange in Halifax. Each is to carry a local Metro fleetname in the style Metro Leeds, Metro Halifax etc. A few buses are repainted but the scheme is abandoned before the PTE comes into being and a new fleet-wide verona green and cream livery is adopted. The local Metro names are retained.

South Yorkshire adopts a new livery of cream with a coffee coloured roof and skirt, a combination which is even less exciting than it sounds and which the PTE is noticeably slow in applying. This replaces off-white and blue in Sheffield, a mainly blue livery in Rotherham, and an attractive red in Doncaster, where the livery had been designed by a local art college.

Coventry, whose predominantly Daimler fleet is absorbed by West Midlands, generously sets municipal pride to one side and starts repainting buses in PTE and cream from the beginning of the year, in advance of its annexation. The enlarged Greater

The new look at Midland General, with NBC poppy red on an ageing Lodekka in Nottingham. Midland General's buses had previously been blue and cream.

Manchester PTE which takes over from Selnec, acquires Wigan's all-Leyland bus fleet. Greater Manchester retains Selnec's orange and white livery but with different shades of both colours to counteract problems with fading paintwork.

Proponents of electric power believe, as they have always done, that there is a breakthrough in battery technology just around the corner. Before becoming Greater Manchester, the Selnec PTE takes delivery of a full-size battery-powered Seddon which proves to be no more practical than any others of its type with a combination of limited range and high unladen weight.

A more successful Seddon enters service with the Scottish Bus Group. It is a Pennine VII, powered by a mid-mounted Gardner engine and fitted with an Alexander Y-type body. SBG orders more before the year is out — almost 100 for 1975 delivery — but the Pennine VII, which can best be seen as a Gardner-powered Leopard, finds few other buyers.

Aside from the takeovers and amalgamations brought about by local government reorganisation, there are other smaller business acquisitions during the year. Midland Red purchases Harper of Heath Hayes, whose fleet includes venerable ex-London RTLs. Cleveland Transit acquires Saltburn Motor Services, and with it a fleet of assorted Bedfords. National Travel South West acquires Wessex Coaches of Bristol and introduces the Wessex National name. The newly-created West Yorkshire PTE moves into the coach business in a big way by buying the Hanson business in Huddersfield.

Minibuses are in the news, even if they're not being taken very seriously. Five Ford Transits are introduced to a dial-a-ride service in Harlow, operated by London Country Bus Services and financed by the Transport & Road Research Laboratory and the local councils. London Transport introduces a similar service in Hampstead.

In 1974 there's a Commercial Motor Show, which is still held in the cosy confines of London's Earls Court. Bristol shows the VRT3 with Leyland's unpopular 510 engine. It has sound encapsulation to cut noise levels. A supposedly low-noise Fleetline chassis for London, the B20 with turbocharged Leyland 690 engine, is also on show. Leyland, struggling to find sales to support its recently-opened Workington factory, shows a Leyland National Lifeliner ambulance. It's a fine idea, but a blind alley.

Alexander launches a new dual-purpose body, the T-type, and the first is at the show in the livery of the Tyne & Wear PTE's Galley coach fleet. The T-type is to win orders from SBG, which is hardly surprising, and it will also manage to pick up a few from NBC too. A bus which might be ahead of its time (a tactful way of saying few are sold) is the Alexander S-type, an integral midibus based on Ford A-series units. Duple shows a new and attractive Dominant bus body.

NBC poppy red did not always wear well, but it could sparkle on a newly-painted bus, such as this 1971 Alexander-bodied Atlantean seen in Cardiff in 1974 after its first repaint.

Above:
The Merseyside PTE area was expanded and the entire fleet was painted green. This is a Liverpool division bus, an Alexander-bodied Atlantean, seen prior to the 1974 boundary and livery revisions.

Below:
Southport became part of Merseyside. A typical Southport PD2 in the town centre just days after the change shows the new Merseyside name applied over the town's municipal crest.

This is a time when Britain's two major bus groups announce bulk orders. And NBC's 1974 requirement is big. It orders nearly 1,650 vehicles of which almost 500 are Leyland Nationals and just over 500 are double-deckers. There are also over 100 Bristol RE coaches, but this is the last year that NBC buys REs. When it announces its orders for 1975 all of its coaches will be Leyland Leopards. This rate of fleet renewal equates with a 12 year vehicle life.

The smaller Scottish group's orders are correspondingly more modest, and for 1974 delivery it ordered 289 buses and coaches, all single-decked and all but 29 to be bodied by Alexander. The absence of double-deckers is brought about by a combination of circumstances — the group's ambivalence towards rear-engined vehicles, the work progressing on the new Ailsa, and supply problems with the Fleetlines which it would have ordered if it did go for 'deckers. A short-lived enchantment with lightweight Fords sees the type appearing in fleets which have not previously tried them.

The new vehicles for both organisations are replacing time-expired buses delivered in the late-1950s. Although rear-engined buses have been around for 15 years, conventional crew-operated half-cab 'deckers are still a common sight, with the last examples being just five years old. The need to dispense with conductors to cut operating costs is helping speed their replacement.

NBC is buying Nationals because it has a financial interest in the Leyland National factory. SBG is not

Darwen Corporation was absorbed by neighbouring Blackburn. A PD2 pulls out of Darwen's small bus station in the last days of Darwen municipal operation.

Doncaster Transport had an unusual livery layout with well-designed lettering for fleet names and other details. This was lost in a brand new image created for the South Yorkshire PTE. A Roe-bodied Daimler CVG6 demonstrates the Doncaster look.

buying Nationals because it doesn't like rear-engined buses. Elsewhere the National makes limited headway. There are some in London, which is currently just a bit suspicious of single-deckers after the criticisms which its standee Swifts and Merlins have attracted. Selnec has a number, and the first new buses for South Yorkshire are Nationals. In Scotland there are a few running for independents. But large sections of the industry regard it with some apprehension. It doesn't have a Gardner engine. The 510 power unit is turbocharged — which adds complexity — and it's noisy. You can't choose your own body with all the little foibles which builders like Northern Counties and East Lancs will willingly accommodate — indeed Leyland National is none too keen even to let you have a bus with a two-colour paint scheme.

Leyland is making it clear that the writing is on the wall for its other single-deck models. The Panther is dead (and unlamented), the Swift is dying, and the RE is to be made available only to export markets. It's a move which wins Leyland no friends, even if the durable National structure is forecast to have a 20-year life.

While British-built AECs, Leylands, Bedfords and Fords are far and away the most popular choice for independent coach operators, a new name is appearing in some well-known fleets: Volvo. Volvo first appeared in the UK in 1972 with an unlikely B58 demonstrator fitted with an Alexander Y-type body. At the start of 1974 there are 45 B58s in operation in Britain. By the end of the year the figure has passed the 100 mark, all bodied by Duple and Plaxton, and

Right:
National Travel, with its all-white coaches, was looking to Europe in the early 1970s with the launch of a service to Frankfurt. The cream of the Tillings Transport fleet, an ECW-bodied Bristol RE, pulls out of Victoria Coach Station in London, bound for Frankfurt.

Volvos are running in such well-known fleets as Park of Hamilton (in a sombre black livery), Glenton of London (with centre-entrance bodies), Hills of Tredegar and Trathens of Yelverton.

British-built bodywork is still the order of the day. Caetano bodywork from Portugal has an established, if somewhat limited, following with its rather garish styling. Van Hool is showing interest in the British coach market, but the British coach market's response is to show little interest in Van Hool. The coach of the year at the Brighton rally is a surprising vehicle — a Willowbrook-bodied Bedford YRT from the fleet of a small Kent operator, The King's Ferry.

Hindsight may frequently be used in conjunction with rose-tinted spectacles. But whatever problems the upheavals of 1974 may have caused Britain's bus operators, it wasn't really a bad time. And viewed from a distance of 20 years it looks to have been a very good time indeed.

A small number of independents were buying new double-deck buses in 1974. These included OK Motor Services, with this attractive Northern Counties-bodied Atlantean.

Municipal fleets renamed in 1974:

Old name	New name
Aberdare	Cynon Valley
Accrington	Hyndburn
Burnley, Colne & Nelson	Burnley & Pendle
Burton on Trent	East Staffordshire
Llandudno	Aberconwy
Lowestoft	Waveney
Lytham St Annes	Fylde
Pontypridd	Taff Ely
Swindon	Thamesdown
Teesside Municipal Transport	Cleveland Transit
West Monmouth	Islwyn
Widnes	Halton

The South East Lancashire North East Cheshire PTE was renamed Greater Manchester, whilst the Tyneside PTE became Tyne & Wear.

Municipal fleets amalgamated in 1974:

New fleet	Fleets absorbed
Blackburn	Blackburn and Darwen
Lancaster	Lancaster and Morecambe
Rhymney Valley	Bedwas & Machen, Caerphilly and Gelligaer

Municipal fleets absorbed by PTEs in 1974:

Fleet	Absorbed by
Bradford	West Yorkshire
Coventry	West Midlands
Doncaster	South Yorkshire
Halifax	West Yorkshire
Huddersfield	West Yorkshire
Leeds	West Yorkshire
Rotherham	South Yorkshire
St Helens	Merseyside
Sheffield	South Yorkshire
Southport	Merseyside
Wigan	Greater Manchester

NBC new bus and coach orders for 1974 delivery:

Double-deck	
Bristol VRT/ECW	344
Leyland Atlantean/Park Royal	174
Total	*518*

Single-deck	
AEC Reliance/Duple	32
AEC Reliance/Plaxton	66
Bedford Y/Duple	34
Bedford VAS/Duple	2
Bedford VAS/Plaxton	1
Bristol LH/ECW	148
Bristol LH/Plaxton	6
Bristol RE/ECW coach	65
Ford R/Duple	47
Ford R/Plaxton bus	20
Leyland Leopard/Duple	82
Leyland Leopard/Marshall	50
Leyland Leopard/Plaxton	74
Leyland Leopard/body not announced	15
Leyland National	488
Total	*1,130*
TOTAL	**1,648**

SBG new bus and coach orders for 1974 delivery:

Bedford Y/Alexander	15
Bedford Y/Duple	5
Ford R/Alexander	59
Ford R/Duple	24
Leyland Leopard/Alexander	185
Seddon Pennine VII/Alexander	1
TOTAL	**289**

Left:
Sheffield Transport was the biggest constituent of the new South Yorkshire PTE. Among the vehicles which passed into PTE ownership was this 1963 AEC Regent V with Weymann body.

Below left:
Among the first buyers of MCW's new Metropolitan was Leicester City Transport.

Top right:
The Leyland National was gradually becoming more commonplace, and the first examples for London Transport were running in 1974. They carried on attractive livery with white roof and yellow entrance doors.

Bottom right:
The West Monmouthshire Omnibus Board's fleet remained unchanged, but the operation got a new name in 1974: Islwyn Borough Transport. A 1970 Willowbrook-bodied Leopard pulls out of Pontypridd on the last day of West Mon operation.

Below:
Glasgow Corporation had already given way to the Greater Glasgow PTE in 1973. Buses which retained the old corporation livery were given GG logos, as shown by an Atlantean in the city centre in 1974.

A LIFE OF BRIAN

Stagecoach has grown from a motley collection of second-hand buses into a truly international giant. **Gavin Booth** tells the story so far . . .

Once upon a time there was an accountant named Brian. And if that seems a boring start to a fairy story, it gets better. Brian was interested in buses (see, I *told* you it got better), and while he was studying he worked as a conductor for Central SMT.

Now in the good old days Central made money. Operating in the industrial heartland of Lanarkshire — this was in the 1970s when Lanarkshire *had* an industrial heartland — Central regularly made as much money as the other six Scottish Bus Group companies put together. As a conductor, this can hardly have escaped Brian's notice.

Brian Souter had other connections with the bus industry. His father, Iain, drove for Alexanders (Midland) in the family hometown of Perth. Brian's older sister, Ann Gloag, had gone into the self drive motor caravan business as Gloagtrotter in 1976 and moved into minibus rental with the purchase of a secondhand Ford Transit.

It was 1980, a significant year for the British coach industry. As a first step towards total deregulation, express coach services no longer needed licences from 6 October that year. Although the express coach market was not large, the recently-elected Conservative government was testing the water as a

prelude to the major upheavals that were to come. The government saw the deregulation of express services as a means of unleashing hordes of frustrated entrepreneurs on to the market. In practice there were few entrepreneurs waiting in the wings and fewer still who lasted the pace.

Brian had joined sister Ann in Gloagtrotter. They bought a couple of full-size coaches for contract work in Perthshire, and then in the summer of 1980 father Iain was made redundant by Alexanders (Midland) and ironically his severance pay from this nationalised monopoly went to help his children set up in the free market.

Three days after D-day for coach services, Gloagtrotter started a service from Dundee to London with single fares that substantially undercut the equivalent SBG fare of £11.50. At first the service ran only at weekends, overnight, but soon there were more frequent departures, and the starting-point was extended northwards to Aberdeen.

Gloagtrotter's first large vehicles were a mixed bunch of secondhand acquisitions — two Bristol MWs, a Leyland Leopard and a Volvo B58. As well as the GT Coaches name that had been adopted, the Volvo was christened 'The Stage Coach', believed to be the first sighting of a name that has become familiar throughout Britain and in other parts of the world.

The first new coach for the company was another Volvo, a late-model B58, with one of the first Duple

In the early days Stagecoach concentrated on running long-distance coach services with a fleet of Neoplan Skyliners. STEWART J. BROWN.

Stagecoach expanded in Glasgow with a fleet of Routemasters serving two perimeter housing schemes. This operation was sold to Kelvin Central in 1992.
STEWART J. BROWN.

Dominant III coach bodies, the small-windowed design developed for the competing SBG services between Scotland and London; Stagecoach somehow managed to get one of these before SBG deliveries began.

The first venture into what was still called stage carriage operation was in 1981 when the Perth-Errol service of A&C McLennan of Spittalfield was taken over; these were still the days when almost the only way to get into the stage carriage market was to buy from established operators. The rest of the McLennan business followed late in 1985, giving Stagecoach more premises in Perthshire including the Spittalfield depot that was to become a graveyard for all manner of company vehicles.

Back in 1981, and the transport establishment was beginning to take note of this Scottish upstart. At first there had been tolerant amusement among the soberly-suited executives in Britain's bus company boardrooms. They smiled at Stagecoach's presumption. Imagine this little Scottish company taking on the might of the establishment. And what a silly name — visions of cowboys and all that. They'll be out of business by Christmas. It'll all end in tears.

Why, the boss didn't even wear a *suit*. He wore casual clothes, allegedly *red* shoes, and carried his business papers in a carrier bag. Good grief, he's still in his twenties!

But the cut-price fares were having an effect.

Traditionally coach travel between Scotland and London had been the cheapest end of the market, appealing to those travelling on a budget — students, the unwaged, older people travelling alone. Now they could get to London, perhaps less comfortably, but in much the same time and save a few quid.

So SBG joined the coach fares war and for a while everybody seemed to benefit. Passenger loadings improved all round and customers (as passengers were now described) got better coaches and cheaper fares.

Other operators noted the apparent success of Stagecoach and competitors came and went, but for many it was the appearance of the Neoplan double-deck coaches that really put the company on the map. Brian and Ann bought their first Skyliners in 1982 and branded them 'Super Stagecoach' — a new level of service which included 'in-flight' snacks, prepared by other members of the Souter family. The big Skyliners were not the company's first double-deckers. These were Bristol Lodekkas bought in 1980/81 which wore a new livery of white with blue, red and tan relief, not quite the current Stagecoach livery, but going that way.

Cumberland's Kendal bus station briefly became a dumping ground for withdrawn buses in the late 1980s. In the front row are a Southdown PD3, a Hampshire Bus Leopard in overall white, and a sad-looking one-time Midland Scottish Leopard. Routemasters lurk in the background.
STEWART J. BROWN.

The Bristol LH was never a common type in Scotland. Bluebird Northern runs seven in the Inverness area, with Inverness Traction fleetnames.
GAVIN BOOTH.

There were stories at the time of a rich uncle in Canada who was pumping money into the fledgling Stagecoach. The sums involved reportedly varied from thousands of pounds to millions. It was a good story in the best *Sunday Post* tradition — uncle emigrates, makes good in oil business, helps struggling Davids to take on the nationalised Goliaths. The basic story was true, though the sums of money were greatly exaggerated. Frazer McColl did take a stake in Stagecoach and this certainly allowed Brian and Ann to expand the business without too many borrowings.

A further cash bonus came in the summer of 1982 when British Rail — or rather the National Union of Railwaymen — helped Stagecoach and other coach operators with a drawn-out rail strike.

The Stagecoach fleet could still be counted on the fingers of several hands, as the spectacular expansion was a few years off, and, although local acquisitions boosted the numbers, the total fleet still hovered around the 50 mark.

The Scottish Bus Group created its Scottish Citylink brand late in 1983 and this heralded a period of more aggressive competition on Scottish and cross-border services. But while Stagecoach was still essentially an

express coach operator it was quietly developing its Perthshire school and service work, and laying plans for the forthcoming deregulation of local bus services. Former London Routemasters started to appear in Perthshire in 1985, the first real use of these buses outside London and northeast England, and the start of an RM revival in which Stagecoach would play its part.

For local bus deregulation Brian and Ann set their sights on Glasgow, Scotland's largest city and a well-ordered transport network with Strathclyde Buses running principally within the city boundaries and various SBG companies providing the out-of-town services. Stagecoach set up a new company, Magicbus, to operate its new Glasgow services; there were three of these — one to the overspill new town of East Kilbride, and the others to the immense peripheral housing estates of Castlemilk and Easterhouse. RMs were widely used on these services and although the East Kilbride service was quickly abandoned the others continued, and the sight of Easterhouse-bound RMs roaring along Glasgow's urban motorway was to be a familiar sight for some years.

Deregulation also allowed expansion in Tayside in competition with a newly-formed SBG company, Strathtay. But Brian and Ann were looking at a wider stage. The sale of National Bus Company subsidiaries was now under way and the word was that there were

bargains to be had. Stagecoach bid for City of Oxford, without success, but every sale attracted a mix bag of bidders so nobody took their interest too seriously. The sober-suited businessmen amused themselves with images of red shoes and plastic bags.

It wasn't quite so amusing when Skipburn successfully bought Hampshire Bus in 1987, for Skipburn was a company formed by Brian and Ann with Frazer McColl — yes, the Canadian uncle — and Dawson Williams, managing director of Hampshire Bus. It definitely wasn't funny at all when Skipburn bought Cumberland Motor Services three months later. After six months the HB Southampton operation was sold to Solent Blue Line, and Stagecoach concentrated on the Andover, Basingstoke and Winchester areas.

There were other unsuccessful bids in 1987, but before the year was out Stagecoach Holdings Ltd

Below:
Dual-door buses acquired from Northern Scottish are used on local services around Aberdeen. They are Alexander-bodied Olympians.
GAVIN BOOTH.

A long way from its original owner, Central Scottish, this Y-type bodied Leopard came to East Midland from Maun Buses. It is seen in Doncaster.
STEWART J. BROWN.

(which had absorbed Skipburn) had bought United Counties. In just a year it had its quota of three NBC companies, and had boosted the fleet by over 700 buses.

The buses inherited were a typical NBC mix: Leyland Nationals, Leopards and Olympians, Bristol VRs and some LHs, a few Tigers and a number of minibuses. For a time the fleets continued outwardly unchanged but soon there were signs of Stagecoach influence. Cumberland got some RMs for service in Carlisle; Hampshire Bus was to have got some but never did; United Counties got a batch for Bedford and Corby.

Stagecoach had been buying new coaches since 1981, but with three sizeable companies now within the fold, the first of a regular series of orders for full-size buses was placed, and 30 long Leyland Olympians with Alexander bodies were ordered for 1988 delivery.

Then in 1988 it was announced that the Scottish Bus Group companies were to be sold off and Stagecoach indicated its intention to bid for them all, although under the sell-off rules it could buy only two.

A threat to Hampshire Bus came when Basingstoke Transit was formed by Harry Blundred to operate minibuses in the town. Blundred had led the first successful buy-out of an NBC company with a bid for Devon General and Stagecoach responded quickly to this threat by dispatching a fleet of Leyland Nationals to provide a free service in Torbay, right in Blundred's Devon heartland. Writs flew, so Stagecoach withdrew and ended up buying Basingstoke Transit.

It seems likely that a further consequence of the Torbay affair was the purchase of 47 late-model Bristol VRTs from Devon General's increasingly minibus-dominated fleet. These, and growing numbers of existing vehicles, plus the new Olympians, were painted in the now-familiar Stagecoach corporate livery of white with orange/red/blue stripes. This was largely to facilitate the transfer of vehicles between fleets, something that started to happen almost as soon as the company started to expand and has continued at a bewildering pace.

Centre right:
Stagecoach operations in Scotland expanded with SBG privatisation. A Bluebird Northern Olympian loads in Fraserburgh for Aberdeen.
STEWART J. BROWN.

Bottom right:
Large numbers of new minibuses have been bought, with Alexander bodywork on the Mercedes 709D emerging as the standard. This is an Inverness Traction example in Dingwall.
STEWART J. BROWN.

Now the Stagecoach horizons were even broader. Stagecoach International was formed to handle overseas projects, and Speedybus Enterprises Ltd was formed to operate former Hong Kong double-deckers in China.

The most significant overseas development in 1989 was the purchase of United Transport International's 51% stake in United Transport Malawi, later to become Stagecoach Malawi with fleet additions in the shape of ERF Trailblazers and some former Hong Kong double-deckers. More recently Stagecoach Malawi has received purpose-built double-deckers — Dennis Dragons with Duple Metsec kit bodies assembled by PEW Bodybuilders, a local firm in which Stagecoach has a shareholding.

Looking back, 1989 was a particularly important year for Stagecoach. Other purchases that year included three former NBC companies which were bought from their managements following completion of the NBC sale. First was East Midland, then came Ribble and Southdown, and to add to the mix came Portsmouth Citybus and Inverness Traction. Not a bad year.

There were sales too. East Midland's separate Frontrunner South East business, formed to operate London area contracts, went to Ensign Bus; Frontrunner North West went to Drawlane along with Ribble subsidiary Bee Line Buzz plus most of Ribble's Manchester area operations. Part of the deal to buy the troubled Portsmouth Citybus operation involved the transfer of the Southampton-Winchester service to Southampton Citybus.

More Olympian/Alexanders followed in 1989 including three on three-axle chassis, with seats for 96 (two for Cumberland) or 110 (the Megadekka for Magicbus).

Minibus replacements include Ivecos with Robin Hood and Phoenix bodies for United Counties in 1988-90, and Reeve Burgess-bodied Ivecos for East Midland, but subsequently large batches of Alexander-bodied Mercedes 709s have been ordered.

The Inverness Traction acquisition reflected a reawakened interest in Scotland. Earlier in the year a concerted campaign had been waged against SBG's Strathtay company in Perth, with Stagecoach Perth Panthers competing on an increasing number of Strathtay services. After several months of fighting, agreement was reached in early 1990, which reduced the pressure on both operators.

The situation in Inverness was different. Inverness Traction had been set up in 1988 as a minibus operator to compete with SBG's Highland Scottish, but after difficulties had sold out. Stagecoach started with a mixed bag of minibuses but soon introduced its standard Mercedes-Benz 709/Alexander buses on the Inverness services and mounted an audacious coup in 1991 when the newly-privatised Highland company was facing staff problems and buses were drafted in, literally overnight, to compete on Inverness town

services. Today Highland is a shadow of its former self, and IT very much the dominant Inverness operator.

For many the most surprising event in 1989 was the sale of the Stagecoach express operation, plus vehicles and the Walnut Grove premises in Perth, to National Express. This was what had started Stagecoach off in the bus and coach business and the sale was an indication that the company's future lay principally in local bus operations.

New names in 1989 were Stagecoach South (combining Hampshire Bus and United Counties) and Stagecoach North West (Cumberland and Ribble). Stagecoach Scotland was formed in 1991 to combine the Inverness, Tayside and Glasgow area companies.

Another overseas purchase was the Canadian coach operator, Gray Coach Lines, bought from Toronto Transit Commission, but more recently in trouble following problems over disputed maintenance payments.

The activities of Stagecoach seemed to be of particular interest to the Monopolies & Mergers Commission, especially over the purchase of Portsmouth Citybus. After MMC investigation Stagecoach was ordered to sell the company, and early in 1991 Harry Blundred's Transit Holdings took over.

The first Stagecoach success in the SBG sell-off was Bluebird Northern, based in Aberdeen, and after a legal battle, Fife Scottish followed a few months later.

A surprising move in 1992 was the sale of the Glasgow-based Magicbus operation to former SBG company Kelvin Central Buses, now employee-owned. There was conjecture that this was to clear the Stagecoach feet to buy Strathclyde Buses, but in the event SBL went to its management and staff. We shall probably never know how many attempts Stagecoach

Three Dennis Javelins with Duple bus bodies were evaluated by Hampshire Bus. They were later transferred to Ribble, but their performance won Dennis an order for 50 Javelin chassis
STEWART J. BROWN.

The standard Stagecoach double-decker in the late-1980s has been the long-wheelbase Olympian with Alexander body. A Cumberland example is seen when new in Carlisle, pursued by a minibus still in Cumberland colours.
GAVIN BOOTH.

has made to buy other companies. Certainly many approaches have been made, often purely speculatively, and there was the very public campaign to ensure that, if West Midlands Travel could not be bought, then it should be sold at a proper commercial price.

At the same time name changes were taking place on the south coast. Southdown's western area became Sussex Coastline Buses, and the rest of the company plus Hastings Buses became South Coast Buses.

There has been more expansion in Africa with the purchase of majority shareholdings in Kenya Bus Services and Kenya Bus Services (Mombasa) from

Recent additions to the fleet have included over 100 Dennis Darts with Alexander Dash bodies. These can be seen from Portsmouth in the south, to Inverness in the north. Magicbus in Glasgow received a number shortly before the operation was sold to Kelvin Central, whose fleetnumber is carried on this bus.
STEWART J. BROWN.

ET, and even farther afield, Wellington City Transport in New Zealand. Nobody believes that this will be the end of the Stagecoach group's global acquisitions. Brian Souter has said that the opportunities in the UK are limited, whilst overseas, particularly in those countries which are implementing privatisation and/or deregulation, there is a bright future.

Of course the UK acquisitions have not stopped. The latest, as this was written, was the Alder Valley company, now renamed Stagecoach Hants & Surrey.

In little more than a dozen years Stagecoach has grown from a motley selection of secondhand coaches into a truly international transport group with well over 3,000 vehicles and 11,000 staff, and a pre-tax profit of £7.7m on a £140m turnover (1991/2 figures).

The sober-suited businessmen now take Stagecoach very seriously indeed. Brian still wears red shoes and is rarely seen in a suit, but nobody cares. He and Ann have built up a successful business from an unlikely base. They have been able to approach the bus business at a time of change with a clean sheet; they have refused to accept ingrained practices and customs; they have peeled away layers of admin and

ride of the fleet? A trio of tri-axle Olympians was purchased - two for Cumberland and one for Magicbus in Glasgow. They remained Britain's only three-axle double-deck buses.

Inter-company transfers are a feature of Stagecoach. Bluebird Northern runs Mercedes minibuses transferred north from operations on the south coast of England.
GAVIN BOOTH.

engineering staff; their lieutenants are some of the most able people in the industry.

The Stagecoach objectives are simply stated: to maximise profit margins at all existing operations, and to acquire undervalued or underperforming companies where they can identify the potential to improve operating margins to at least 15% of turnover.

In achieving all it has done Stagecoach has not always made friends. There are many enthusiasts who dislike the corporative livery and regret the passing of traditional schemes like Fife's red and Southdown's green, but there is no mistaking a Stagecoach bus — in Kirkcaldy, Brighton or even Nairobi. There are the neighbouring operators who fear the might of Stagecoach, but events have shown that Stagecoach fleets will jealously guard their territories and hope that other operators will, too. Of course there have been the more aggressive exercises like Inverness and Perth, and incidents like the Torbay free buses indicate that Stagecoach will not sit back and tolerate incursions into its territory.

More than any of the other post-NBC supergroups, Stagecoach has supported the UK bus manufacturing industry with regular orders. With a mixed inheritance from NBC and SBG, fleet replacement has been a priority. Large fleets of Leyland Olympians, Dennis Darts and Mercedes-Benz 709s have been bought, mostly with Alexander bodies, and as I write Volvo B10Ms are entering service with Cumberland, and the first of 90 Plaxton-bodied dual-purpose vehicles are being delivered (60 on Volvo B10M, 30 on Dennis Javelin). The overseas fleets have also received deliveries to their operating conditions.

But Stagecoach is not just a bus operator. The birth of Stagecoach Rail in 1992 was an early indication of interest in British Rail's privatisation. And the group has looked at light rail.

Things move fast in the Stagecoach empire. This story is being written early in 1993, but by the time you read this, up to a year later, the group may well have grown, often in the most unexpected ways and in the most unexpected places. As well as British Rail privatisation there are the London Buses subsidiaries to come on to the market, and there has long been an interest in Ulsterbus.

Brian's enthusiasm is unbounded and infectious. He takes the business seriously, but not himself. There is something refreshingly cavalier and unstuffy about the way the group is run. Like the semi-official sweatshirts that are prized by some staff. On the front is the word STAGECOACH; but on the back in the style of rock concert souvenirs are the words WORLD TOUR 1985-1992 and a list of conquests, starting with McLennans in 1985 and finishing with Mombasa in 1992. This had barely been produced when Alder Valley came into the fold, and there will doubtless be more versions to follow.

The sweatshirts are white, but the lettering is in red, probably to match the shoes.

THE SPANGLES FACTOR

London Country's operating territory encircling the
capital was once described as the mint with the
hole. **Alan Millar** asks where it has gone.

Do you remember Spangles, those tubes of
individually wrapped square boiled sweets? Perhaps
you had a favourite flavour. One of the fruits, maybe,
acid drops or the distinctive Old English variety
beloved of lunchtime drinkers who tried to overlay
their alcoholic breath with something equally pungent.
You can't buy them any more. I've no idea when it
happened, but sometime over the past 20 years Mars
withdrew them presumably because they were losing
their appeal.

Much the same has happened to London Country
Bus Services. One day, it was the biggest National
Bus Company subsidiary, running close on 1,200
buses and coaches. Almost the next day, it seems, it
has all but vanished, broken up, sold off and reduced
to tiny shadows of its former self. You could call it the
Spangles Factor.

London Country, in fact, lasted only 16-and-a-bit
years, but its disappearance has swept away a much

London Country started off with an ageing fleet inherited from
London Transport. This 1965 Routemaster coach counted among
the more modern vehicles, although by the time this picture was
taken in Croydon it had been demoted to bus duties.
STEWART J. BROWN.

longer legacy of London Transport history. Its fate
may well hold clues to what will happen when London
Buses is broken up, privatised and exposed to
deregulation.

Created with only £2 share capital to take over
London Transport's country buses and Green Line
coaches in January 1970, after the rest of LT was
transferred to Greater London Council control, it
inherited one of the most awkward operating
territories in the country. The so-called 'mint with a
hole' area surrounded, but did not include London,
took in the new towns of Stevenage, Hemel
Hempstead, Harlow and Crawley as well as some
bigger towns like Guildford, Slough, Watford and
Dartford, but also thinly scattered green belt
communities with high car ownership levels.

Some say NBC ought to have broken it up among
other subsidiaries, but it was a unique entity, with a
fleet of largely old LT buses, LT wages and working
conditions and LT restrictive practices which would
have sat uneasily in the like of United Counties,
Maidstone & District or Eastern National. Instead,
LCBS got the heavy treatment, including a head office
at Reigate in Surrey and central workshops at
Crawley. The inheritance of RTs, RFs, GSs and

Routemasters was replaced with the buses closer to NBC standards, notably over 500 Mk1 Leyland Nationals and nearly 300 Atlanteans, as it converted all its services to one-person operation. Even newer LT-standard Swifts and Merlins had gone by the company's tenth birthday along with other Swifts acquired through NBC.

The cross-London Green Line coach network, strangled by traffic congestion and staff shortages, got new leased coaches from 1977, lost its worst performing routes, was focused on more promising markets like the airports and tourist attractions and grew with the commuter coach revival which followed the first phase of deregulation in the early-1980s. Fifteen Olympian double-deck coaches were bought for commuter and airport routes, supplementing 73 Olympian buses bought after NBC stopped buying Atlanteans.

LCBS was also scoring points off its old owner, picking up contracts to run supported services in

Left:
Almost 20 years later SuperBus lived on in Stevenage route numbers in 1991. But in a world where marketing leads, Sovereign has fallen behind and there's little that's super about a Leyland Olympian nudging ten years old.
ALAN MILLAR.

Below:
Green Line was upgraded by London Country with fleets of new coaches bringing unprecedented luxury to the express network. New routes with their own brand names - this is Flightline - were added. The coach is a Duple-bodied Leyland Leopard.
STEWART J. BROWN.

urrey which had previously been provided at far greater expense by London Transport. And when LT returned to state control in 1984 as London Regional Transport and it was obliged to start putting the red bus route network out to tender, LCBS was extremely well placed to succeed. Not only were its costs lower than London Buses' but, unlike most independents, it had a network of depots strung right round the outskirts of the capital. To start with, it met these new commitments with its existing fleet, appending rear route number boards to meet LT's more exacting destination requirements for tendered routes, but it was soon buying about 70 secondhand Atlanteans from within NBC and from Greater Manchester and Strathclyde PTEs.

But time was fast running out for LCBS. Even before the 1985 Transport Act, which deregulated the bus industry and privatised NBC, received the Royal Assent, NBC had sealed its fate. By dividing Midland Red up into smaller operating and engineering companies in 1981, it had turned LCBS into its largest subsidiary and set in train a series of similar sub-divisions of companies across southern and western England. Closest to LCBS, United Counties, Alder Valley and Maidstone & District all were treated this way and early in 1986 the then Transport Secretary, Nicholas Ridley, ordered NBC to break up its four biggest companies, Ribble, United Auto, Crosville – and LCBS.

Only seven weeks before deregulation, four operating areas to which many day-to-day responsibilities had been devolved since 1979 began their new existences as separate companies with the cumbersome titles of London Country Bus (North West), (North East), (South West) and (South East), with headquarters in Watford, Hertford, Reigate and Dartford and fleets of between 200 (South East) and 400 (South West). The Crawley works became Gatwick Engineering.

The management teams had little time to get to know one another, never mind fully understand the harsh new world in which they were expected to work or prepare to buy their companies from NBC. And, while LCBS had been able to compete in London with out-of-town costs, the LT legacy of higher wages and restrictive practices – and of big brick-built garages –

meant the new companies' costs were high compared with those of others moving in on many of its main markets. In the haste to eliminate losses, more routes were deregistered in some places than could be won back in the tendering process, opening up opportunities for competitors to expand.

The South East company was the first to break completely with its old identity, relaunching itself early in 1987 as Kentish Bus with a maroon and cream livery designed by bus livery specialist Ray Stenning's Best Impressions company. North East was actually the first to give itself a new image, adopting a new two-tone green and white livery soon after its formation.

All five companies remained in NBC ownership throughout 1987 and had to be advertised separately to try and generate more interest from potential buyers. North West was the first to go and was the 48th sale in the privatisation programme. Its management team paid £3.7 million in January 1988, gaining operations spread from Slough to Watford as well as the Green Line name which was still being used by the other three companies.

Gatwick Engineering was sold the following month for only £800,000 to Frontsource, the company headed by former NBC privatisation consultant Robert Beattie which had already bought up six other regional engineering companies and Alder Valley in one of the more controversial parts of the whole privatisation programme and was selling on some of the property at a substantial profit. Gatwick Engineering and five of the other companies were sold to the Bus Engineering Group, headed by two Frontsource managers at the beginning of 1989, but it went into receivership 18 months later and the Crawley works closed.

Kentish Bus fetched £2.4 million in March 1988, £800,000 less than its book value, when it was bought by Proudmutual, the company formed by management at Northumbria Motor Services to buy that company (a product of Nicholas Ridley's compulsory break-up of United Auto) five months earlier.

To help sell the loss-making South West and North East companies, their operations and property were sold separately. A Leeds development company, Parkdale Holdings, bought both companies' property. Drawlane Transport, set up to buy NBC companies by a group of businessmen led by Wiltshire entrepreneur Ray McEnhill, bought South West's operations to add to Shamrock & Rambler, North Western and Midland Red North. It later closed Shamrock & Rambler and bought Crosville, Bee Line Buzz and Midland Fox from their initial owners.

North East, the last NBC bus company to be sold, went in April 1988 to the AJS Group formed by East Yorkshire's then chairman, Alan Stephenson, to buy West Yorkshire Road Car the previous year and which had just bought control of Premier Travel's coach and bus operations. Parkdale had also bought West Yorkshire's property. The South West sale fetched £3

million from both buyers, North East £3.6 million; in both cases more than the book value of their assets.

North East's problems seemed to be the most acute of all the London Country companies. Rock-bottom morale before the sale had led to a series of strikes, during which it lost its three contracts for LT tendered services. It had also attracted some particularly potent competition – Harris Bus in Grays, Jubilee in Stevenage and Sampson's of Hoddesdon in Harlow. Groups of disenchanted drivers had also left to start their own minibus companies, Welwyn Hatfield Line in Hertfordshire in 1987 and Buzz Co-operative in Harlow in October 1988.

It was also under attack from another ex-NBC company. Luton & District, part of the old United Counties, had been bought by its employees in August 1987 for a mere £1.7 million and was bent on expansion. It was winning tenders against London Country (North East) and, in the aftermath of the industrial disputes, bought the Green Line Flightline service from Luton airport to London Victoria. North East's Olympian coaches were soon shipped north to East Yorkshire which was then still part-owned by Alan Stephenson.

More drastic action clearly was required and the AJS way was to break its big companies up into smaller business which could then be made viable. It would later become clear that this also turned them into more manageable bite-size chunks for others to buy.

So, just as West Yorkshire was split initially into three subsidiaries with small company cultures, London Country (North East) was split in two from January 1989. The western half became Sovereign Bus & Coach, painted its buses blue and cream and adopted fleetnames of Stevenage Bus and, at Hatfield and St Albans, HertsRIDER. The eastern half became County Bus & Coach, with a green and cream livery in the same corporate style not only as Sovereign but of AJS's Yorkshire fleets, and traded with local names

Centre left:
Despite privatisation, the NBC-inspired green livery was long-lived. This former LCNW Atlantean is seen in Watford in 1991, still in NBC livery but with Luton & District's fleet name on the front.
ALAN MILLAR.

Bottom left:
LCNW's livery was maintained by Luton & District after it bought the company from its managers. A Leyland-bodied Olympian operates on a London Transport tendered service.
STEWART J. BROWN.

f Townlink in Harlow, Lea Valley at Hertford and Thameside at Grays. Each had about 100 buses at formation, with about 70 older vehicles, mainly early-1970s Atlanteans, being sold off in an auction.

Sovereign and County, like other parts of the lost LCBS empire, were fighting with the wrong weapons. In NBC days, Atlanteans had been drafted on to the new towns routes to provide extra capacity, but low frequency services with high cost buses were no match for new competitors' high frequency minibuses. Both companies bought their own minibuses to fight back and many of their double-deckers were either sold or shipped north. Several of County's 27 ex-LCBS Olympians were sold to Wilts & Dorset or transferred to AJS's Keighley & District, where the corporate livery meant only the green bits needed to be painted red; and Sovereign's 12 newest Atlanteans were sold to Yorkshire Rider in 1989 shortly after it bought part of West Yorkshire from AJS. County also got Leyland National 2s from Yorkshire fleets and Sovereign more recently has swapped Olympians with Keighley for more Lynxes and has taken ex-West Yorkshire VRs for school contracts.

AJS's chequebook bought out several competitors. Sovereign took over Jubilee almost at its formation, with Jubilee's Metroriders and Leyland Lynxes joining its fleet and some Duple-bodied Leyland Tigers going to County which bought out Sampson's in March 1989, absorbing its bus operations and keeping the coach business as a separate trading unit. And in January 1990, Welwyn Hatfield Line was bought out, kept as a separate company but managed by Sovereign. A bid to buy out Buzz Co-op fell at the last hurdle, but after the two operators agreed to a truce in their battle of Harlow.

Sovereign and County both managed to re-establish themselves in the LT tendered market, where the other ex-LCBS companies were making inroads, too. Sovereign got into Harrow in 1990 with a package of routes run with 27 Reeve Burgess-bodied Mercedes-Benz midibuses, a type it has also bought for other of its and Welwyn Hatfield Line's services. It set up a separate subsidiary, Sovereign Buses (Harrow), to run the LT services and used Sovereign as a fleetname for the first time. County won a wider range of services, operated with a mix of midibuses and big buses, Lynx (AJS's standard single-decker) and Northern Counties-bodied Olympians.

But more changes were afoot. Parkdale had served notice for the companies to quit most of the prime town centre depot sites and, although the property slump would leave most of them vacant long after the last buses moved out, this did help the companies find lower cost bases. The acquisitions of 1989 had helped, too, as freehold depots came with both Jubilee and Sampson's. County moved most of its Hertford buses to Hoddesdon, but the Stevenage business was too big for the Jubilee site.

But not long after Luton & District made its next move. Anxious to expand further, it tabled an offer AJS could not refuse and in May 1990 bought two thirds of the Stevenage business including rights to the Stevenage Bus fleetname and the Cambridge-London Green Line service. Forty-two vehicles (21 Nationals,

London & Country expanded into central London on tenders. An East Lancs-bodied Volvo Citybus approaches Trafalgar Square. STEWART J. BROWN.

six Olympians, two Lynxes, five Metroriders and eight Tiger coaches) went in that deal. And it wasn't all that AJS was selling.

The bulk of Premier Travel went at the same time to Cambus Holdings and Bob Howells, managing director of AJS's South of England Travel Group, the holding company for Premier and the ex-London Country businesses, set up Lynton Travel to buy County from AJS. The deal was phased to raise the necessary finance, with some services from Grays being managed by County, but owned by an off-the-shelf AJS company until the end of 1990 when most of them were bought by County. But the most expensive new buses, 14 Olympians leased for LT route 103 in the Romford area, went with the route to Grey Green.

Since then, County has expanded further in the LT tendered market, buying more Mercedes and Plaxton and Wrights-bodied Dennis Darts and in September 1992 eliminated another competitor when it bought the bus operations of Golden Boy of Roydon, a long established independent in the Harlow and Hertford areas. In less than four years, its fleet had virtually doubled in size.

Sovereign has changed hands, too. In 1991, as Alan Stephenson prepared to sell the last of his bus interests, it looked like an overseas buyer would move in. CNT Holdings, owner of Hong Kong Citybus, had just bought Ensign Bus, was relaunching it as Capital Citybus and was keen to expand it. Sovereign's mix of LT contracts and new towns services seemed attractive at first, but not at the prices asked by AJS. Instead, it was bought by Blazefield Holdings, a management buy-out within AJS which also bought the remaining Yorkshire operations and, later in the

As its fortunes have risen and fallen, so has Kentish Bus changed its vehicle policy, sometimes buying secondhand buses and disposing of relatively modern vehicles. This Olympian came from Northumbria Motor Services.
STEWART J. BROWN.

year, Cambridge Coach Services, the company formed by AJS to take over Premier's services from Cambridge to London and London's airports, and the associated Rover Coaches of Bromsgrove.

Cambridge Coach Services is managed by Sovereign Buses (Harrow) which has also taken over some services in Watford. The HertsRIDER fleetname has been dropped, with Sovereign's name used exclusively.

London Country (North West) survived only 34 months as an independent company. Although it managed to pick up two LT contracts, requiring 15 Olympians and eight Dennis Darts, and it expanded minibus operations with Renault S56s and MCW Metroriders, it never overcame its financial problems and in October 1990 it too succumbed to an attractive offer from Luton & District. The deal, which virtually doubled the size of the Luton company, retained the green and grey livery adopted by North West after privatisation, but little else.

Its head office administration and most of its top management went, the buses somewhat irrelevantly acquired Luton & District fleetnames on the front and legal lettering on the sides and, as a symptom of the new owner's devolved management structure, local fleetnames replaced the London Country names. Now, just as there already were Luton Bus, Dunstable Bus, Hitchin Bus, Aylesbury Bus, Stevenage Bus and Red Rover names on the red fleet, the green buses sport Hemel Bus, Slough Bus and Watfordwide fleetnames. Another operator already used Watford Bus, so Luton had to resort to Chiltern Buses, a name used by LCBS in the early-1980s after a Market Analysis Project route revamp. The Slough operations were sold to Q-Drive in February 1993 and merged with that group's Bee Line business.

And thanks to the demise of two municipal companies, the fleet has been purged of its Atlanteans. Highbridge ECW, East Lancs and Alexander-bodied Series 3 VRTs were bought from Lincoln City Transport, after employee-owned Derby City Transport, in which Luton & District has a 25 per cent stake, bought 40 per cent of the Lincoln company. These joined some ex-Cambus Series 2 VRTs in

Centre left:
LCNE adopted a two-tone green and white livery which was short-lived. This is a Roe-bodied Olympian.
P.E. ROWLANDS.

Bottom left:
LCNE was split into two companies by its new owners, AJS. This is a Sovereign Bus & Coach Olympian with HertsRIDER name.
P.E. ROWLANDS.

Slough and allowed the Atlanteans to be sold to Maidstone & District as it moved in to kill off the last of Maidstone Boro'line's operations.

The better part of Boro'line, 57 buses (Olympians, Scanias, Volvo Citybuses, Lynxes and some Minibuses) used on LT tendered routes in the Bexleyheath area and other parts of southeast London, were taken over by Kentish Bus in February 1992 in a move which pushed Boro'line into receivership and led to buses being painted out of one Best Impressions livery into another.

Kentish Bus had done well in the LT market, with double-deckers and Metrorider midibuses, and had set up an additional base north of the Thames, at Hackney, to handle routes in Docklands and into central London. Proudmutual ownership is betrayed by Newcastle registrations on many of the newer buses and by ex-Northumbria Olympians moved south for contracts in the Woolwich area. Olympian coaches went north in exchange. Extra life has been squeezed out of some of the ex-London Country Nationals by having them rebuilt by East Lancs as National Greenways for LT contracts, but the small fleet of Scanias went to Nottingham in 1992 and some newer Olympians were sold to Drawlane companies after the loss of other contracts.

Drawlane, meanwhile, has taken its knife to the South West company. It negotiated its way out of many of the demarcation practices which added to its engineering costs and cut these costs further by replacing its oldest buses, many of which were moved to Manchester and the group's equally troubled Bee Line Buzz company. The 120-odd replacements, many for LT contracts in south London, were a mix of Volvo Citybuses, Dennis Dominators and single-deck Falcons and Leyland Lynxes, many with bodywork by East Lancs, which Drawlane bought from the John Brown group in January 1988; for routes in some of

the Surrey towns, it has bought Northern Counties-bodied Renault S56s, the group's standard minibus. In 1991, it rebuilt the first National Greenway in conjunction with East Lancs and has more recently bought several ex-County Nationals for Greenway conversions.

It closed five of the nine garages acquired by Parkdale and moved into a new £6 million depot in Croydon in 1990, one of the very few new depots built since the industry's upheavals of 1986.

Outwardly, the biggest change has been to the identity of the company. It was relaunched in April 1989 with yet another Best Impressions livery and given the trading name of London & Country, underlining the two markets it serves. The drab ex-NBC livery was replaced by a much brighter two-tone green and red. And it has expanded westwards.

That opportunity came in the autumn of 1990 when, as part of a refinancing of the Q-Drive group, Drawlane bought the Surrey half of Alder Valley (Q-Drive had bought the whole company from Frontsource two years earlier) with depots in Guildford, Woking and Cranleigh, renamed it the Guildford & West Surrey Bus Company and began to paint the 48 buses – ten Alexander-bodied Olympians, the company's first five Bristol VRTs, 21 nationals and 12 minibuses – into London & Country colours. There was a strong chance it could have gained Alder Valley's Hampshire operations two years later, but Drawlane was out-bid by Stagecoach.

But a smaller acquisition within Drawlane had been made earlier in the year when it took over 13 elderly Nationals operated by TGM Buses on two LT routes in west London. TGM was the bus operating wing of Tellings-Golden Miller of Byfleet which, in the sometimes Byzantine ways of Drawlane, is a coaching subsidiary of Leicester-based Midland Fox. The appearance of the smoky and noisy Nationals in Hounslow High Street had excited local opposition, not least from one of the leading councillors, none other than Dave Wetzel, former high profile chair of the GLC Transport Committee and implementer of the popular cheap fares policy of the early-1980s. Remember him? There also appeared to have been problems in meeting LT's service quality levels, hence the takeover, but the services continued to be run largely with the same buses in TGM's blue and white livery.

They add yet more variety to a fleet which has lost its old colours more slowly than most of the other bits of London Country. In mid-1992, not only were there still buses in NBC green, but Shamrock & Rambler colours could still crop up when least expected.

The other part of LCNE became County Bus & Coach. It was sold by AJS and has expanded in LT tendered operations in north and east London, mainly with new Dennis Darts. Plaxton Pointer bodywork is fitted to this one.
P.E. ROWLANDS.

Another part of the business had been hived off in October 1989 when Drawlane created Speedlink Airport Services to operate the Speedlink and Jetlink express services between the London airports as well as some National Express contracts, and which – yes, you've guessed – also uses Best Impressions liveries. This had been one of the newest and most successful developments of Green Line and in Drawlane's view it needed to be managed by a specialist company which would not allow its standards to be compromised by bus operation. Equally, it allowed London & Country to get on with running buses.

Two years later, after Drawlane had acquired a 25 per cent controlling stake in National Express, Speedlink was sold to National Express to form a vital part of that restructured business as Ray McEnhill and fellow Drawlane director Adam Mills prepared to leave Drawlane and float National Express on the Stock Exchange.

By contrast, the rest of Green Line was close to breathing its last. LT found itself short of cash in 1991, partly because the recession had decimated the value of its property assets, and support for seven Green Line routes was axed. Most were replaced by commercial bus services, but one was reprieved. LT awarded London & Country a short-term contract to run the Dartford-Heathrow 726 link across southern London and put the route out to tender. London Coaches, in the throes of being sold by London Buses to its managers, won the contract and leased ten dual purpose Ikarus-bodied DAF SB220s to run it. Their red Best Impressions livery extinguished another of the traces of LCBS.

Otherwise, save for a few commercial commuter and tourist services, some of which only carry the Green Line name on windscreen boards, Green Line like LCBS, is just history. The 'mint with the hole' has gone the way of all Spangles.

LOOKING AT LOTHIAN

Edinburgh is one major city where the main operator survived the upheavals of deregulation in 1986 remarkably little changed. **Graeme Yuille** illustrates Lothian Region Transport in recent times.

For many years Edinburgh's standard bus was the Alexander-bodied Leyland Atlantean with panoramic windows. The penultimate batch of AN68s was delivered in 1979.

Lothian runs a varied single-deck fleet. Twelve Leyland Leopards with Alexander bodies were delivered in 1976. They were replaced by Leyland Lynxes in 1991. A Leopard runs along George Steeet on a tendered service.

The biggest fleet order for Leyland's Cub to come from a bus operator was a batch of 18 for Lothian. These had Duple Dominant 31-seat bus bodies and after deregulation could be found helping to fight competition, as seen here at Trinity in 1988, where Lothian was under pressure from Eastern Scottish. The Cubs were built at Leyland's Bathgate factory.

Two Leyland-powered National 2s were delivered in 1984, bringing the fleet total to eight. The Nationals were delivered in this attractive livery layout - this one is running on a post-deregulation route to destinations outside Lothian's traditional city-based operating area.

A further 12 National 2s were purchased in 1985. The Nationals have acquired a simpler, traditional livery when falling due for repaint.

Right:
When Leyland discontinued the Atlantean, Lothian switched to Olympians, standardising on long-wheelbase chassis. Between 1983 and 1986 four batches of Eastern Coach Works-bodied Olympians joined the fleet. All have Leyland TL11 engines.

For the airport coach service Alexander supplied six Olympians with single-doorway bodywork fitted with 78 coach seats.

From 1988 the body order for the Olympians was switched to Alexander and power was supplied by Cummins following the cessation of Leyland engine production. A 1988 bus descends the Mound.

Competition on sightseeing tours prompted Lothian to convert four elderly AN68s to open-top. An astonished tourist on the top deck stares in disbelief at the sun shining on Edinburgh, ignoring the world-famous Castle atop the hill behind her.

In 1991 Lothian received its first Leyland Lynxes. These were 12 Cummins-powered versions of the new Lynx II and were the first production dual-door Lynxes. They were also the last. At the end of 1991 Volvo announced the closure of Leyland's Workington factory and the end of Lynx production.

Lothian's long-standing loyalty to Leyland has yet to be successfully challenged. One would-be challenger has been Scania. Scania's N113 demonstrator with Alexander body was tried in service by Lothian in November 1990.

BUSES I MIGHT HAVE BOUGHT

Robert E. Jowitt muses on bus preservation and missed opportunities

If I am to discuss the buses I might have bought but didn't buy I should perhaps explain how and why, as I am not a bus operator, I came to consider the question of buying buses at all. I will accordingly begin with a brief account of how I came to be in such a position.

The idea of preserving old vehicles was familiar to me from my early youth, when my father was vociferous in a campaign to save Wantage Tramway locomotive No 5 and, at a time when support from public bodies was extremely poor, toyed with the notion of purchasing the loco himself. I wish he had (though it now resides, perhaps more suitably, in the GWR museum at Didcot).

My first acquaintance with the buses of Paris — which later were to play a major part in my life — came not long after the Wantage episode when a French family visited us and brought me a prewar Dinky toy open-platform bus; this type of vehicle, said my father, was a delightful and typical feature of Paris.

We move on to the late 1950s, when the Bournemouth evening paper informed its readers they could, for £60, buy one of the mid-1930s Sunbeam trolleybuses which were now starting to be withdrawn. It was a nice notion, but what could you do with a trolleybus? And I didn't have £60. I rescued a number plate from the scrapyard near Weymouth where they were broken up, instead.

I first visited Paris in 1960, and instantly fell in love with the open-platform Renault buses, which were already give-or-take a quarter of a century old and many of them to a design which looked far older. The first one I photographed was No 3267, which has some relevance hereafter, although then it was just one bus among many. A year later, near Valenciennes, I encountered a Paris bus in service as workmen's transport, and its driver told me all about it. If he could buy one, so could I, and accordingly I wrote to the RATP. They sent me sale notices and specifications, but problems such as insurance and finance proved insuperable. The next bus which caught my fancy was a very choice Tilling Stevens of unknown origin but possibly from Bournemouth; much of its number plate

1936 Sunbeam MS2/Park Royal Bournemouth trolleybus BRU21 seen in the Square in 1960. A year or so earlier some of her 1935 sisters were for sale at £60 each, but what could you do with a trolleybus? This one was the youngest of the batch, and at 24 years old still looked ageless. Behind is an ex-Brighton BUT/Weymann.
ALL PHOTOS BY ROBERT E. JOWITT.

Top:
A retired garden shed from near Tiptoe on its way to the scrapyard. If the person engaged on removing it had been present Jowitt might have tried to buy it. Fortunately, perhaps, it was unattended. It is a c1930 Tilling Stevens. Part of the number plate is broken off, but it may well have read LJ (Bournemouth), as its garden shed days were spent only ten miles thence; possibly therefore it was one of many express coaches which fought for London traffic in that era.

Above:
Jowitt could distinguish King Alfred's No 103 by telepathy from her two identical sisters long before he could see the number plate - even when diverted by dolly birds. This scene is in the salubrious suburb of Teg Down.

was missing. It had lingered for many years as a garden shed between Ashley and Bashley, on the road to Tiptoe (yes, really) on the southern fringes of the New Forest where I was then resident. I never visited the bus in the garden — it was one of those things I could always do tomorrow — and then suddenly it materialised on a layby near Ashley. It proved to be in utterly deplorable condition and presumably was on its way to a breaker's yard. Had there been anyone in charge of it I believe I would have negotiated with them on the spot in an attempt to have it taken instead to our garden. Then the whole course of my life would have been very different. But there was no one with it and the next day it was gone.

In the next couple of years I turned my attention to late-1940s Triumph roadsters, those lovely cars with huge headlights and a dicky seat — finance again proving a stumbling block — and Harrods battery-electric vans. Harrods Transport Manager was extremely helpful and this scheme might have come to fruition save that, because I wanted to keep it in Harrods livery, the higher ranks of Harrods turned it down for fear of 'misrepresentation'.

Another trip to Paris convinced me that my first idea was the right one, and I continued to hope against hope. Returning to Paris again in 1969, not knowing if any open-backed buses were still running, I was enraptured when a 1935 TN4F came swinging round the corner to tell me there was still some soul in the city. Checking up afterwards, I found that the bus which greeted me was none other than No 3267. This was Fate; come what might I must acquire it. By now I was acquainted with knowledgeable people such as George Behrend and Prince Marshall, advice was forthcoming and I was earning a certain amount of money.

On my next visit to Paris I had the satisfaction of seeing my name against No 3267 on the list of vehicles reserved for disposal when withdrawn, and meanwhile could ride on the bus which would one day be mine. In June 1970 she became mine. In January 1971 to keep her company, I acquired a 1936 TN4FH 3380, the last traditional open-platform to operate.

It was suggested I had bought two to breed. They did. Two years later I bought No 2679, a 1933 TN6A which was already in England but unloved by its owners, and 15 years after that No 3489, another

Love at first sight . . . and only sight and last sight. Speeding through Nantes on a gas and electricity workers' special, Compagnie Nantais des Transports en Commun No 216 was, in September 1972, one of the last survivors of the formerly widespread pug-nosed - or as the French called them, pig-nosed - Chausson APH model of the late-1940s.

TN4H again from English owners, very unloved and in lamentable condition which I hope in time to rectify.

To return to the early-1970s . . . Flushed with the success of being the owner of two buses, and regardless of the many attendant problems, I felt I might very well have more; and apart from those two Parisiennes just mentioned I engaged in the pursuit of several buses, and it is of these 'might have beens' that I will now write.

It was at this period that I returned to live in Winchester where I had spent my childhood. My fancy was at once taken by the King Alfred Motor Services, to which I had never paid a lot of attention previously, preferring steam trains. But King Alfred buses were splendidly independent, and green and cream like Paris buses. My favourite soon became Leyland Tiger Cub No 103, which I could distinguish at a great distance from its sisters Nos 104 and 105. I can only suppose that was telepathy. I asked if I could buy it at such time as it was withdrawn, and this might have come about had not King Alfred been taken over by Hants & Dorset in April 1973. I transferred my request to Hants & Dorset, and again it was agreed to; and with No 103 likely to be withdrawn at any moment, the likelihood of my purchase was such that

the bus was actually attributed to my ownership in a handbook of preserved buses. Price comes before a fall; and Hants & Dorset's right hand knew not what its left was doing — the bus was sold to another. It worked briefly as a bus in Wimbledon, went on to become transport for a sports club, then became a horsebox somewhere in the wilds of Hertfordshire. From there it was stolen and partly broken up before its owners recovered it. They were at that time in negotiation with the Friends of King Alfred Buses, who had already rescued No 104 from a South Welsh bus company. No 105 had long since been cannibalised for spares by Hants & Dorset, being uneconomic to repair. By this time I felt that Fate had counted me out of the game and I was content to let the Friends take on the sad remains of No 103 to break up for spares for No 104.

Meanwhile on a trip to the continent in 1972 I had discovered quite a selection of buses that I felt I could not live without. In Nantes, I saw one of the original late-1940s Chaussons — the sort with a pug nose. These had been abundant in France ten years earlier but were now a rarity. This one was in the Nantes city fleet, most of which consisted of the later round-fronted Chaussons, also very typical, and fairly desirable too — in the same sort of way as cheap French red wine.

Further south, in Clermont Ferrand, there were some three-axle Berliets which I remembered new in 1960, now looking rather the worse for wear. They were enormous vehicles, and if they had only 20 or so seats, they were allowed to carry over 100 standing passengers. Mostly they worked in large cities such as Lyon and Marseille and I suppose their purpose in Clermont Ferrand was to carry Michelin workers.

Somua OP5/3 of the late-1950s still has slots to hold Parisian route boards and a frame for Parisian advertisements - and inside it still has its RATP fleet number 385 - when working for the Transports des Bouches du Rhône at Arles in 1972. Its new owners, having removed its Parisian route number box and painted it red and cream, considered it thoroughly up-to-date and were probably affronted by the idea of it as a candidate for preservation.

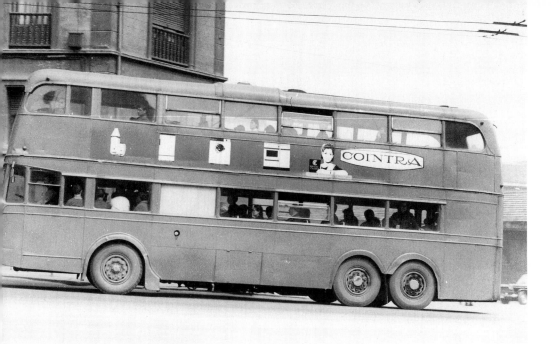

A masterpiece in splicing. Running under trolleybus wires, but no longer a trolleybus, this is one of a pair of London BUT 'Q1' trolleybuses converted by Bilbao, Spain, to diesel operation with Leyland Worldmaster engines and with bodywork lengthened over the front axle by a window and a bit. This one is seen in 1969, in all-over red of the same shade as LT.

South again, in Arles, famed for its beautiful Grecian-like girls, was another highly desirable vehicle. This was an ex-Paris Saviem OP5/3 of c1955 still retaining its RATP fleet number inside and generally original, except for being red and cream instead of green and cream, and having lost its route number box. It belonged to the Transports (formerly Chemins de Fer) des Bouches du Rhône who, even if they still ran goods trains, transported their passengers by bus. It is true that the Saviem OP5/3 buses were never as marvellous as their prewar companions, but they had a charm of their own, and on account of their large windscreens they had an even more tragic canine expression than the dog-like faces which were such an endearing feature of the Renaults. And, with its scarlet sides and its Arlesienne aura, this specimen had an extra allure.

On over the border into Spain, Bilbao, like several other Spanish cities, boasted a fleet of ex-London trolleybuses. According to the whims of their operators and the necessity of changing to driving on the right, these were all cut about and altered in one fashion or another but none more so than two of the Bilbao fleet, Nos 277 and 287. These had an extra length spliced into them ahead of the front axle, so they were one window and a bit longer than originally built, and probably as big as the Berliets . . . and double-deck besides!

Furthermore, they had been converted from trolleybuses to diesels, with Leyland Worldmaster engines and were thus a more practical proposition for preservation than the trolleybuses; and at the same time they had retained a London Transport shade of red livery and bell buttons saying 'push once', so they had the best of both worlds.

So much so that I went to the bus depot, where an amiable person in authority assured me, with a gold toothed smile, that he would put my name down by Nos 277 and 287 and let me know the moment one was withdrawn. Perhaps he was at the dentist when it happened or perhaps he thought he would write to me *mañana* or perhaps he had lost my address. When I passed through Bilbao some years later, there was no sign of my trolleybuses or of Nos 277 or 287. I didn't go to the depot to find out what had happened. I felt again that Fate had not meant me to have it. It is sad, but I must admit that my sadness was tempered with some relief, for by then I'd had some experience of bringing a three-axle bus home from the continent, as you shall shortly see.

Inspired by what seemed like successful negotiations in Bilbao I wrote to Nantes, Clermont Ferrand and the Transport des Bouches du Rhône, expressing an interest in acquiring the various vehicles. The Bouches du Rhône replied shortly that they had only just acquired the Saviem themselves, it was as good as new and they had no intention of parting with it. Reading between the lines I had the impression they thought I was confoundedly cheeky. I didn't return to Arles for another 17 years, by which time the Bouches du Rhône, and presumably the Saviem, had vanished from the face of the earth in a regional bus reorganisation.

Nantes, on the other hand, agreed that their Chausson was indeed something of an antiquity and were prepared to discuss the matter further in due course.

Clemont Ferrand said nothing for a while, then, suddenly, in 1973 a firm of second-hand commercials in Lyon said they were disposing of some of the Clermont vehicles and if I wanted a Berliet I must make haste to Clermont and collect it. By now I had my third Renault, and was doubtful about taking on something else, but a friend of mine said he would be interested if I could fetch it, and if it could be parked at the farm where two of my Renaults were; and he might even pass it back to me later. So I set out for Clermont Ferrand, telling Nantes I would call in to discuss the Chausson on the way back. At Clermont Ferrand I drove the Berliet up and down the yard a few times. It had grown enormously since I had last seen it, but I felt I could manage it. I had been proposing to travel via Aubusson, to head for Nantes, but the men at Clermont Ferrand advised me against it. They said the road was too mountainous. Perhaps they had the Berliet's tyres in mind. It was sold without its contract tyres and obviously therefore shod with anything that happened to be lying around; a fairly rough collection it is true, but good enough to get it to Cherbourg. So I set out northwards. It was fine on the open road, but the passage of a couple of lesser provincial towns decided me firmly against trying to pick my way through the maelstrom of traffic in Nantes, and to head direct to the coast via as few conurbations as possible. I spent the first night in an extremely comfortable hostelry with the Berliet parked on the village green.

The next day's journey was uneventful but the next evening I couldn't find anywhere except the floor of the bus to sleep. On again next morning into the Cotentin peninsula and roads I knew quite well. I was feeling pleased with my progress, and thinking I would be in Cherbourg in good time, when the bus suddenly slewed sideways and I found myself charging onwards with the bus tilted over at an angle of 45°, the nearside wheels in a ditch, the brakes not responding and all my maps and worldly goods cascading over me from the rack above my head. For a moment the bus leapt back to its rightful angle as it crossed a field approach, and then back to half over, and finally slithered to a stop. The countryside which had been completely unpopulated a moment before was soon filled with red-faced Northern farmers all agape. I will not dwell on the complications which ensued save to say that when the bus was finally pulled from its resting place the nearside tyre on the forward rear axle was discovered to be even more agape than the admiring Normans, who were eagerly reciting to the several British motorists in the resulting jam that the bus had been supposed to be going to a museum in England. It was being towed into a garage yard in Coutances while I departed ignominiously in a service bus for Cherbourg wondering whether I would ever see it again.

My friend's first reaction was to scrap it, for not only would it need a new tyre, but also the brake pipes had been torn off the bottom by the edge of the ditch. I prevailed upon him to have it repaired; and, when this was done, prevailed upon the garage to deliver it to Cherbourg, so that I might drive it straight on to the ferry. But when I found it in Cherbourg docks I also found its parking lights on and its battery flat. This was naturally on a Saturday evening, and during the rest of that evening and the following morning I learnt thoroughly the French art of *se débrouiller* which is roughly, though inadequately, translated 'to muddle through'. I booked in at a hotel then went to a restaurant. The good *patron* of *Le Grand Balcon*, on hearing my woes, sent me off with his sons and a friend and a car and a spanner. With much labour we abstracted the four batteries and took them to a garage where they were put on charge. The next day was Sunday, and snowing, and the *Grand Balcon* boys had gone off for the day. My hotel manager lent me a spanner, I got a taxi, the taxi driver watched me load the batteries into the taxi, watched me unload them at the docks. By some miracle, or at least by having charged batteries, the bus started; but the fun wasn't over. The customs men demanded various papers of which I had never heard — and never been asked for when exporting the Renaults — and fetched some headman who told me not to leave the customs house while he went to see about it. After an endless wait he returned and grudgingly said he might arrange it if the bus corresponded with such papers as I had. He

In the depot yard at Clermont Ferrand in 1973, the three-axle Berliet PBR of 1960 waits for its journey to England, alongside several rather older and equally desirable and scrappable Chausson APH.

crawled all over the bus and finally decided it did. I drove on to the ferry. Five minutes later the gangway was pulled up. I felt I was now fully qualified to speak not only of the term *se débrouiller* but also that of 'piehead jump'.

But my troubles were not yet over. I passed the Southampton customs with no more than the usual hassle they employ on lunatics who import scrap buses, but only a mile from the docks, I was stopped by a police car. 'Your bus,' the officer said, ' is making so much smoke that I can't read the label that says Burleet on the back.' I forbore from asking how he knew what it said if he couldn't read it, and from the further refinement of saying that actually it is

pronounced Bear-lee-eh, and explained that it had just started from the docks after several cold hours on a ferry, and that the smoke would soon diminish (though privately I doubted it). After complaining about the absence of trade plates he was satisfied with the English insurance I had taken out specially for this journey and mutteringly allowed me to proceed with it, back to the farmyard. My friend came down to admire it and cleaned it . . . once. After two or three years the farmer began to be a bit annoyed at the limited access to his dung heap. Had I taken it on myself it would have continued limiting access to the

Clermont Ferrand Berliet in a Normandy ditch. *The Sapeurs-Pompiers* (fire-brigade) are considering how best to get it out. The field gateway over which the bus had for a moment reverted to its normal attitude in its headlong dash to destruction is visible beside the towing vehicle. The Norman farmers keep their vigil from the hedge.

dung heap. It was sold to some enthusiasts from Southend, who took it away on a low loader, and I have never heard of it since. For all I know it may still be in Southend. Despite its many problems I can't help hoping it is. But you may begin to see why I went no further with the Bilbao ex-trolleybus or even with the Nantes Chausson; I'd had enough.

This apart, lack of parking space was a problem. After the farmyard was abandoned, my three Renaults were parked tight into a Winchester suburban garden. The fourth, when I bought it, had to sit several miles away with the vehicles of the Friends of King Alfred — my wife flatly refused to have a fourth bus in the back garden — especially a derelict bus. When we left Hampshire for Herefordshire our choice of house was considerably influenced by the fact that the property had to include suitable accommodation for four buses. We found a lovely four-bay barn with a nice house to go with it.

This barn must surely be the final answer to my expansionist notions. And anyway most, if not all, of the buses I might have bought are certainly no longer obtainable. But, as readers of *Buses Yearbook* and formerly *Buses Annual* over the years may have seen, the hatred which I first had for the Saviem Standards which replaced the old French classics has gradually turned to affection. Dare I wonder if there is a little bit of space somewhere to fit one of the now veteran buses which more than 20 years ago pushed my own buses off the road? No, certainly not! What nonsense!

Top:
The buses Jowitt did buy. Seen here over 20 years later, 1935 Renault No 3267 and 1936 No 3380, in a field in Herefordshire. Jowitt was asked: 'Have you got two to let them breed?'

Above:
They did breed. Now there are four, seen here in their luxurious new home in Herefordshire - which has quite a nice house for the family to go with it.

REFLECTIONS

Fotobus is an informal group of enthusiasts whose interest in bus photography extends beyond straight-forward record shots to scenes setting the bus in its environment or, as here, illustrating it unconventionally.

From Mike Greenwood comes a view of a Derby City Transport Ailsa, reflected in a shop window in the city centre.

Left:
Mirrored windows in central Nottingham with a Nottingham City Transport Volvo Citybus and the photographer, Stewart Brown.

Overleaf:
Wyn Hobson spotted this reflective opportunity in Leicester in October 1986. On the right, a Barton Leopard/Plaxton; on the left the reflection of a MIdland Fox Leyland National.

THROUGH THE DRIVER'S EYES

Trent bus driver, enthusiast, and photographer,
John Milnes recommends driving as a career.

Trent ceased to be a National Bus Company subsidiary at the end of 1986, being sold to its management. NBC's poppy red was quickly replaced by a new livery of Ayres red and silver and the company started trading as Trent Buses.

It was a little over 12 months later, at the end of March 1988, that I joined the company and started my driver training at Langley Mill, being put in charge of LRC 454, a 1958 Willowbrook-bodied Leyland Titan PD3. This was a wonderful machine to drive — with correct gear control I could hear the engine sing. I passed my psv test in Derby at the start of April and drove the Titan back to Langley Mill — sadly, for the last time.

After a further week at Langley Mill in the driver familiarisation school I was sent to my home depot, Mansfield. The most memorable experience at that time was coping with the sheer size of a Leyland National, the biggest vehicle I had ever driven, and getting used to driving a vehicle without a clutch. My left leg kept moving as if to say: 'Shouldn't I be doing something?'

At Mansfield the hard work started, and believe me it is hard. While driving, especially in busy town centres, your concentration is 100 per cent on the road. Then at stops you switch your attention to the passengers. To operate competently you have to know all the destinations and fares, recognise the various passes and keep to the timetable. All this has to be learned until it's second nature — and it takes time.

The first new vehicles for Trent Buses were placed in service at the start of 1989 and were 12 Alexander-bodies Volvo Citybuses. Four were allocated to Mansfield and I was fortunate to be allocated one for its maiden service journey. I can remember feeling at ease with the vehicle from the beginning and over the following months they proved to be very trusty workhorses for the company.

They have since been followed by more similar vehicles and by Optare Deltas.

The Leyland National 2 has started to disappear from the fleet, leaving the original National 1 as Trent's standard single-deck vehicle. I know from my experience at Mansfield that the Mark 1 was always more reliable than the Mark 2.

Since deregulation and the increase in competition which has followed, two words have become very important within the company: customer care. A little attention to customers' needs goes a long way, as letters in the local newspapers are showing regularly, though not all passengers appreciate the problems which bus drivers can face.

The biggest problem in the 1990s is the sheer volume of traffic, particularly at rush hours. This leads to late running which can be made worse by road

Trent's Alexander-bodied Citybuses run between Mansfield and Nottingham. One negotiates a tight turn in Kirkby-in-Ashfield in September 1991.
ALL PHOTOS BY JOHN MILNES.

works — or by severe weather. In December 1989 I was running from Mansfield to Nottingham in appalling conditions. The snow was falling heavily, the roads were ungritted, and then as I entered Nottingham the weather suddenly cleared.

I was 45min late and I got some abuse from a lady waiting for the bus in Nottingham. 'Where have you been? Can't you ever operate a service on time?' I suggested that on her journey out she take note of the weather conditions and the heavy snow around Sutton. But when we got there the snow had turned to rain and the road was perfectly clear. She stared at me in disbelief as she got off the bus. 'What snow?' was her parting utterance. Well, you can't win them all . . .

Yet I'd have no hesitation in recommending bus driving as a career. If you can get on well with people, can handle money, enjoy driving and have the strength to lift very heavy baby buggies you'll find it a rewarding job. But make no mistake — it is hard work.

Above left:
Many Trent drivers like the Leyland Olympian. This one is passing through Mansfield on its way from Chesterfield to Nottingham, on a service operated jointly with East Midland.

Left:
Barton was taken over by Trent in 1989. Typical of the older Barton vehicles is this Plaxton-bodied Leyland Leopard seen in Derby in August 1991.

Below:
The National 1 is surviving in the Trent fleet while National 2s are being sold. A National passes a Citybus in Hucknall.

Top:
The number of Bristol VRTs in the Trent fleet is declining. This is one of the Mansfield-based survivors.

Above:
The new order: A Barton-liveried Optare Delta is seen arriving at the 1991 Showbus rally.

91

CHANNEL CROSSING

As European unity comes ever closer to reality,
Kevin Lane looks across the English Channel at
Belgium and France.

A multi-modal interchange in Ostend sees an
articulated tram departing on the coastal
service to De Panne, while a Van Hool
integral bus loads in the background. The
interchange also serves the local railway line
as well as the nearby ferry terminal – a ferry
towers over the docks on the left of the
picture.
ALL PHOTOS BY KEVIN LANE.

*The Société Nationale de Chemins de fer
Vicinaux* (SNCV) operates as *De Lijn* in
Ostend, running both buses and trams. An
elderly Van Hool integral relegated to
contract work stands opposite the tram
sidings. Although better known as *SNCV* in
Britain, the company is abbreviated to *NMVB*
in Flemish-speaking areas.

A picture which demonstrates the new Europe - a French-built coach, owned by an Italian company, on tour in Belgium. The coach is Renault's impressive FR1 integral. The location is Ostend.

In 1988 STCE, the local operator in Calais, was still running a few Belgian-built Brossel BL55s, including this 1969 model with Jonckheere body. Brossel was associated with Leyland and the BL55 had a rear horizontal Leyland O.600 engine and Leyland Pneumocyclic gearbox.

Belgium's flat terrain encourages the use of bicycles, as demonstrated by the cycle park outside Bruges station in August 1992. The bus is a Van Hool integral.

More typically French is this stylish Renault PR100, also operated by STCE in Calais. Renault tried briefly to sell PR100s in Britain in the late 1980s - but only five found buyers. The PR100 was originally produced by Berliet.

Renault developed an articulated version of its PR100 design, the 17.7m-long PR180. The two models have a high degree of parts commonality, but with a more powerful engine in the artic. This PR180 is running for the municipal fleet in Dunkirk.

The German manufacturer Setra, best known as a high quality coach builder, also makes buses. This late-1970s S140 was running in Dunkirk in 1987, operated by STRV, a subsidiary of SNCF, the French railway company.

Unusual French built integrals by CBM - car et Bus Le Mans - are operated in Lille by TCC (Les Tranports en Commun de la Communauté). A line of front-engined TDU-11s load outside the station. The TDU-11 features a DAF engine.

TCC in Lille also runs trams to Roubaix and Tourcoing, with 23km of route. This Duwag articulated car is one of 24 which were previously operated in West Germany, moving to Lille in the early 1980s.

Paris enjoyed a brief flirtation with double-deckers in the 1970s. One Berliet found a new lease of life in Lille as a housing, medical and social security advice office.

NORTHERN CHANGES

Go-Ahead Northern, the largest bus operator in
northeast England, has been through a lot of
changes. **Andrew Jarosz** tells the tale.

Bus service deregulation at the end of 1986, and the
subsequent break up and privatisation of the National
Bus Company, resulted in some considerable changes
to both established operators and newcomers in the
northeast of England.

Northumbria Motor Services appeared as United
Automobile operations north of the Tyne were hived
off to form a separate company. Independents
Trimdon Motor Services and OK Motor Services
registered a considerable number of new routes both
as commercial and subsidised operations.

The former Tyne & Wear Metropolitan County
Council bus company transformed itself into Busways
Travel, with different local identities and liveries.
Many smaller independents ventured into additional
service operations, some of which have now stood the
test of time, with one or two newcomers also springing
up.

The northeast's largest bus company, Northern
General, faced its own set of challenges. With over
300 buses, it was the largest former NBC subsidiary
not to be broken up, yet its operations fell into two
distinct halves.

Services in the Tyne & Wear area were completely
integrated within the County Council route network
and supported by network subsidy, in return for the
loss of a fair degree of commercial autonomy.
Operations in the south and west came under the aegis
of Durham County Council, which though it was no
less supportive, did not insist on items such as
common liveries or pay parity. Northern's problem lay
in re-establishing its identity; indeed some would say
that in some areas it needed to create an identity that
had not hitherto existed. This was because the
anonymous yellow paint that gradually enveloped
every NGT vehicle based in the Tyne & Wear County
from the mid-1970s onward, had actually obliterated
the existence of long-established companies like
Gateshead & District and the Tyneside Omnibus

In the run-up to deregulation Northern painted a few buses in
traditional colours, partly to ensure that the liveries were not
revived and exploited by new competitors. A dual-door ECW-
bodied Atlantean at Beamish museum shows the Tyneside
colours.
GO-AHEAD NORTHERN.

The dark red Gateshead livery on a Roe-bodied Atlantean at Beamish.
GO-AHEAD NORTHERN.

company, which were nevertheless Northern Group associated companies.

Although the company's headquarters and central works are at Bensham in Gateshead, its true roots started in Chester-le-Street in 1913, when Northern General was formed to consolidate BET group tramway and transport interests in the northeast.

Tramway companies included the Gateshead & District, Tynemouth & District, Tyneside Tramways and Tramroads, Sunderland District and Jarrow & District, the first four of which continued as separate bus companies after trams were withdrawn.

After World War 1, Bensham built its own bus chassis, the SE6 and SE4, with the SE6 being the first 30ft single-decker in the UK. Innovatory work continued in more recent times with the conversion of two conventional half-cab double-deck buses to one-man operation by an intriguing repositioning of the driver's cab. The works are now noteworthy as being one of the few central works facilities kept on by any of the major UK bus companies.

National Bus Company bureaucracy gradually forced the poppy red livery on to Northern at the beginning of the 1970s, but Sunderland District blue hung on for a while until NBC decided that only red or green were acceptable corporate colours for its subsidiary fleets. In fact the first Leyland National for the group was delivered to Sunderland District in 1972 and operated in blue and white for some time.

At around this time, the practice of painting buses yellow to harmonise with the PTE corporate image began and the individual liveries of Tyneside (green and cream), Tynemouth & District (red and cream), Gateshead & District (olive green), Venture (yellow and maroon) and of course Northern's maroon began to disappear. Vehicles running outside the Tyne & Wear area thus became poppy red, with the others becoming yellow with one white band and a maroon fleetname. NBC thus allowed one exception to its corporate edict.

During the 1970s the separate companies were put on ice and all the fleets consolidated into NGT. At the beginning of 1975 the Tynemouth, Sunderland and Venture vehicles were integrated, and a year later the Tyneside and Gateshead buses followed. Unless they were specifically transferred out of their area, most of the buses ended their days in the drab yellow livery.

During the early-1980s, when the Tyne & Wear Metro came on stream, the PTE reshaped bus services to complement and feed into the Metro, with a consequent reduction in its own directly-operated fleet. Sixty Leyland Atlanteans were sold to Northern, ten of which had never operated for the PTE, and the all-over yellow livery on NGT vehicles gave way to a

nore attractive yellow and white livery with blue
lining out. At this stage the Tyne & Wear logo took
over on the sides of the buses with the Northern
fleetname usually confined to being displayed on the
front.

The PTE's responsibilities did not end with service
co-ordination. It contributed to Northern's vehicle
replacement programme, paid parity pay to its drivers
to bring them in line with crews working in
Newcastle, and because new vehicles were delivered
in PTE colours, it agreed to pay the cost of repainting
them, should the agreement ever come to an end.

As the debate over deregulation reached its
inevitable conclusion, and abolition of the
Metropolitan County Council became equally
inevitable, Northern had to make plans to establish an
identity, which it had not needed (or been allowed) to
have for some years. During 1985 one vehicle
appeared in each of the former company liveries.

A National appeared in traditional maroon at
Stanley, a National 2 in Sunderland blue and cream,
an Atlantean took on Tyneside green and an Olympian
donned Tynemouth & District colours. In addition
here were two maroon Atlanteans which had
celebrated the centenary of Gateshead Tramways since
1983. Much later, in 1988, a National joined them in
original Venture Transport livery.

Thus NGT was covering its option to return to the
traditional liveries and identities of the past, when

deregulation came. It also protected its position where
any newcomer would find it difficult to start up and
copy the old traditional colours.

Nevertheless the company decided to go for a new
corporate image with a red and white colour scheme
and the Go-Ahead Northern image. When the
metropolitan county was abolished in April 1986,
repaints replaced the yellow with red and there were
even two multicoloured Metrobuses proclaiming
'Don't judge a bus by its colour . . . Read the name!
Go-Ahead Northern, the company that cares.'

The company changed its name to Go-Ahead
Northern and the extremely high profile marketing
established the Go-Ahead image with the public in a
space of less than five years. Administratively, by
1985 it had been split into five districts – Gateshead,
Tyne, Sunderland, Derwentside and East Durham.

The corporate identity, however, could not last
long. By early-1987, faced with the prospect of
lowering its fares to counter opposition from
newcomers, Northern decided instead to introduce a
fleet of orange National 2s which would compete on

The traditional Sunderland District dark blue and white livery was applied to Renault S56 minibuses in the town for a while. An Alexander-bodied example pulls out of Sunderland's covered bus station.
A. JAROSZ.

lower fares on identical routes. At least 17 were painted using an equal mixture of leftover NBC poppy red and Tyne & Wear yellow paint, with the blue previously used for lining out applied to the bus wheels.

Operating in Consett, Stanley, Gateshead, Philadelphia and Sunderland, the buses were at first totally anonymous, with orange bow-tied drivers refusing to reveal their identity. After a while they donned the 'ride the big orange' logo and later still, owned up to begin Go-Ahead Northern vehicles.

The second livery experiment involved bringing back the Sunderland District identity on Minilink routes. A fleet of 21 new Renault S56 minibuses joined a Ford Transit at the beginning of 1988, in a blue version of the Minilink livery at Philadelphia and

Right:
Optare's attractive Delta promotes just the right image for Go-Ahead Northern's Supershuttle service to the Gateshead Metrocentre. The livery is white, yellow, red and blue.
A JAROSZ.

Below:
A post-deregulation ploy was the painting of National 2s in an anonymous all-over orange livery made by mixing left over PTE yellow and NBC red paint. One heads out of Gateshead interchange for the Metrocentre.
A JAROSZ.

Washington depots in a competitive strike which had started with commercial registrations against OK Travel which had captured contracts from Northern.

By 1991, however, management was prepared to admit that whilst the minibus networks were successful in raising patronage, the nostalgia factor had not achieved anything and minis went back into red Minilink livery.

Also in 1988, the coach unit at Chester-le-Street was rebranded with a rich red livery and gold Voyager fleet name for those coaches not employed on National Express duties or in other contract liveries like the Durham Wasps ice hockey team coach. About six higher quality coaches wear these colours at any one time. They were also carried by a 21-seated and wheelchair-ramped National.

Route branding was another departure from the norm. The opening of the Metrocentre shopping complex at Dunston at the end of 1988, brought new opportunities for both Northern and Busways, with Northern providing a car-park shuttle service for shoppers.

Seven National 2s were painted in an eyecatching red, blue, yellow and white colour scheme for the Supershuttle and five of these were replaced by new Optare Deltas in a similar livery during 1990. Some of the displaced Nationals then had the red bands replaced by green and became Festival Shuttle vehicles for the duration of the Garden Festival on the riverside.

A new network of Metrocentre Minilink routes was then introduced from Winlaton with eight Renault S56 minis in a distinctive striped livery together with one

in an advertising livery. After bending under the strain of heavy loads for nearly three years, these were replaced by 14 long wheelbase Optare MetroRiders in similar colours at the end of 1991.

In 1989, Northern won a sizeable contract from the Northumbria Health Authority for the carriage of outpatients and set up a new subsidiary Visitauto which traded as Metro Taxis and Caring Cars. In addition to a number of new black cabs, the company rebranded some Ford Transits as well as additional secondhand purchases into a black, white and yellow livery.

It also repurchased one of its original Nationals from West Riding, which had fitted a ramp and wheelchair anchorages to it. This operated however in the yellow, orange and black livery of Tyne & Wear PTE.

Metro Taxis still operates on a smaller scale, since the loss of the contract, when the Health Authority took it back to its own ambulance service. There are 36 cabs based at Wallsend depot with six minis and four coaches at Percy Main employed on contracts such as night services out of Newcastle. Six Renault minibuses owned by Tyne & Wear PTE are also operated by Metro Taxis on Care bus services.

The Langley Park Motor Co, better known as Gypsy Queen, was taken over in 1989. The company

The Deltas replaced National 2s which were given green skirts and re-allocated to the Festival Shuttle, operated in conjunction with the National Garden Festival, held in Gateshead in 1990. A. JAROSZ.

The Metro Taxis name has been carried on a small number of full-size vehicles, including this Plaxton-bodied Leyland Leopard. The livery is white, yellow and black.
A. JAROSZ.

The first buses to carry Go-Ahead Gateshead names were Optare MetroRiders which were used to serve the huge Metrocentre shopping complex.
A. JAROSZ.

has continued to operate as an autonomous unit with its unique stripy livery, and a new Dennis Dart together with minis and coaches transferred from the parent company have all assumed the livery and identity of the former independent. In 1991 Gypsy Queen was runner-up in the 'Britain's Brightest Bus Company' competition.

Despite succumbing to good commercial and marketing practice in some areas, the bulk of the Northern fleet carried corporate colours and was

Gypsy Queen of Langley Park was acquired by Go-Ahead Northern in 1989 but retains its own identity. It operates the group's first Dennis Dart, a one-off Carlyle-bodied bus. A. JAROSZ.

managed corporately, but by 1990 financial pressures forced Northern management into the view that some depots could no longer afford to offer top wages and conditions, particularly as competitors were paying far less to their staff.

It proposed a new form of depot bargaining which predictably did not go down well with a workforce which had already lost its Tyne & Wear parity pay at deregulation. Nevertheless with redundancies threatened and the more prosperous depots not wanting their conditions to be dragged down by less viable ones, the proposal was eventually accepted.

Below:
The Dennis Dart with Wright Handybus body has come close to being the Go-Ahead Northern group's standard bus, with 65 being delivered in 1992. The first went to the new VFM Buses fleet in South Shields. A. JAROSZ.

South Shields depot staff accepted cuts in wages by autumn 1990 and a new Tyneside Omnibus company was resurrected and the garage started using the South Tyne fleetname either in addition to or instead of Go-Ahead Northern.

By the beginning of 1991 the company was restructured again, with head office staff being reduced and autonomous subsidiaries led by general managers – Gateshead & District, Sunderland & District and Tynemouth & District being resurrected since lying dormant after the big amalgamation in 1975/76. At this time there was still no intention to move away from a corporate livery.

Local identities were added to the fleetname, as the strong brand identity created by corporate livery was felt worth continuing. North of the Tyne, the Coastline identity was added. In the Sunderland area, Wearside in tiny letters was added, whilst in Gateshead the Go-Ahead Northern fleetname was updated with a local motif.

By mid 1991, after an unfortunate strike, thoughts turned to strengthening local identities. It was clear that something new was required in South Shields and rebranding coupled with a comprehensive passenger charter was seen as the way forward.

Two National 2s emerged in a new blue and white livery and, in between being evaluated, competed with another blue liveried independent – Calvary Coaches· of Washington.

The final version emerged at the beginning of 1992 as VFM Buses, with a new image, new vehicles, new passenger charter and lots of new hopes. Having clung for such a long time to its successful corporate identity, Northern cast it off with a vengeance in favour of a two-tone blue livery and a catchy fleetname.

'VFM Buses – means Value for Money' says the fleetname, in an area where the Economic Bus Company fleet identity has recently been enlarged by Busways Travel. The approach is sound enough, if you're not doing too well and your passengers are thrift-minded why not go with the flow? The first 13 Dennis Darts with the Wright Alusuisse body for the group were drafted in at the launch, together with new

return fare bargains and a promise to give better service.

Whether this approach pays off remains to be seen, but it is highly significant that whereas in PTE days double-deckers with 86 seats were required, small 40-seaters will now suffice. The economic reality of an area badly hit twice by recession dictates a new approach.

Rather than turning the clock back, Northern has had the courage to go forward with a new approach, couched in language of the 21st century, and by the end of the year the remainder of the company was rebranded.

Go-Ahead Gateshead followed in February 1992 with its ten new Dennis Darts using a darker red livery but with a dark blue diagonal stripe and an enlarged motif. Not as drastic as VFM's metamorphosis, but still effective. The new fleetname had first appeared at the Bus and Coach Show of 1991 on a new Optare MetroRider.

Northern General, which is now based at Chester-le-Street and also covers Stanley and Consett depots, kicked off in March with the red livery relieved by an additional white band across the wheels in the style of the first 14 Optare Deltas which were delivered in 1989.

It has reverted to the traditional Northern fleetname, which is subtitled 'Proud of our routes'. Once again there is a new passenger charter covering the entire company and the obligatory 15 new Dennis Dart 40-seaters, being joined later by an additional 15. Unfortunately, the traditional 'Shop at Binns' advertisement will not reappear over the front destination indicator!

In the autumn of 1992 a new Wear Buses image with a green-based livery was launched for operations in Sunderland, Washington and Philadelphia – again with a fleet of new Wright-bodied Dennis Darts playing a key role.

The last new identity to appear was Coastline, unveiled at the start of 1993 as red and cream. Go-Ahead Northern has thus become the holding company, with the original Northern General company reverting to its heartland in northwest Durham as one of a number of distinct separate subsidiaries. The wheel may have gone full circle, but the clock hasn't been turned back. We may still have the traditional company names resting on the legal ownership panels of the buses, but there is nothing traditional about the 1993 approach to marketing and delivering service.

Whilst numerous companies have recently gone down the road of splitting into separate cost centres and companies, it seems that Northern's was far more reluctant and less dogmatic. It had the chance to revert to traditional company identities in 1986 but followed the corporate road. It soon became apparent that there was a need to change as the whole climate of public transport was changing. And it's a challenge which Go-Ahead Northern met head on.

SERVING SUTHERLAND

For many years the buses of the Sutherland
Transport & Trading Co provided a lifeline to remote
communitites in the far northwest of Scotland.
Reg Wilson illustrates examples.

Above:
Sutherland Transport & Trading was based in
Lairg and its services connected with trains
from Inverness, carrying both passengers
and mail to isolated communities far from the
railway line. This Albion Victor, bound for
Scourie, was typical of the buses operated in
the 1950s.
ALL PHOTOS BY REG WILSON.

Above right:
During the 1960s small Bedfords were the
mainstay of the fleet. The first of the
company's J4 models had a 16-seat Duple
body with a large mail compartment at the
rear, a characteristic feature of ST&T buses. It
was registered in Glasgow by Bedford's
Scottish dealer, SMT Sales & Service.

Right:
A similar J4, delivered in 1961 and
registered like most of the company's fleet in
Sutherland, loads outside Lairg post office for
Durness on the north coast. The 56-mile run
took around three hours.

Facing page:
In 1962 ST&T switched to Bedford's new VAS2 chassis and had bodywork built by SMT in Glasgow. This 16-seater illustrates the end result, with totally enclosed goods compartment.

Above right:
Most of ST&T's routes operated over single-track roads with passing places. A 1963 VAS2 heads for Scourie in the summer of 1971. Scourie was a two-hour run from Lairg.

Right:
Minibuses played a small part in the company's operations. This Commer 1500 with 12-seat Harrington body was delivered in 1965. It heads out of Lairg with Loch Shin on the left. The ST&T livery was cream and red.

Below:
After buying purpose-built SMT-bodied Bedfords, the company reverted to standard bodies. This VAS with Willowbrook body was delivered in 1973. It still featured a mail compartment at the back.

KENYAN SAFARI

Malcolm Chase recalls the 1970s in Kenya, when Albions and Guys still ruled the roads.

The name Kenya is a word to conjure with – epitome of the British Empire, superb game country or miles of unparalleled beaches.

In 1974 I was fortunate enough to have the opportunity to live in Nairobi and the succeeding five years brought much of interest, not least a variety of buses and bus operating practices somewhat removed from the monotony of the UK bus scene in the mid-1970s.

Kenya had a population then of about 16 million, of whom around 650,000 lived in Nairobi, 400,000 in Mombasa, and 200,000 each in Kisumu (on Lake Victoria) and in Nakuru. By far the greater proportion lived, and still live, in the rural areas, mostly clustered into the fertile regions between Nairobi and Lake Victoria, and along a narrow coastal strip. Other areas are semi-desert, or inhabited by pastoral peoples such as the Masai, or are given over to wildlife.

Typical of the KBS fleet in the 1970s is this 1967 Albion Clydesdale CD25 with ERGW body. Note the full-depth sliding windows and the PSV lettering, a legal requirement, above the windscreen. This bus has an Albion badge; a newer CD25 alongside carries Leyland lettering.
ALL PHOTOS BY MICHAEL CHASE.

Nairobi

Nairobi was founded originally as a construction camp for the railway, on a marshy uninhabited piece of flat land between the Masai plains and the fertile Kikuyu uplands. The name derives from the Masai for 'cold place'.

It is 5,500ft up and despite being only 100 miles south of the Equator has a pleasant climate, not too hot but rather cool in July and August.

The major operator was Kenya Bus Services Ltd, a United Transport company founded by Cdr Hare in 1934, which had a 25% shareholding owned by Nairobi City Council and a franchise expiring in 1985. The former United interest in KBS is now owned by Stagecoach. The fleet reached 166 vehicles by 1971, when 66 million passengers were carried, 240 by 1973 and 290 by 1975. However, owing to increasing competition, the 300 mark was not achieved until 1979.

An intensive service operated on most routes but certain suburban routes were less frequent. Country routes in the 10-20-mile radius had been operated in the 1960s under the Nairobi and District fleet-name; these recommenced in 1980 on a larger scale.

Most routes were through cross-city routes, but some terminated at a bus station opened in 1967, which replaced a more central bus station whose site was acquired for the building of the Nairobi Hilton.

All vehicles were and are based at one large depot at Eastleigh where the offices are also situated.

The livery had been cream, with a thick green band, for many years, but from 1973 the green became two thin bands, later reduced to one. A new general manager in 1974 liked red buses and five were painted in various styles of red and white in 1975. These were not regarded as successful so four then received a yellow/green/white livery in 1976 and three were tried

Deliveries to KBS in the early 1970s featured more comprehensive destination displays. This is a 1972 Clydesdale in the company's Eastleigh depot. All Kenyan registration plates began with the letter K. Note the generous ground clearance.

A KBS (Mombasa) Clydesdale rebodied by Haji Suleiman on a country service at Nakura.

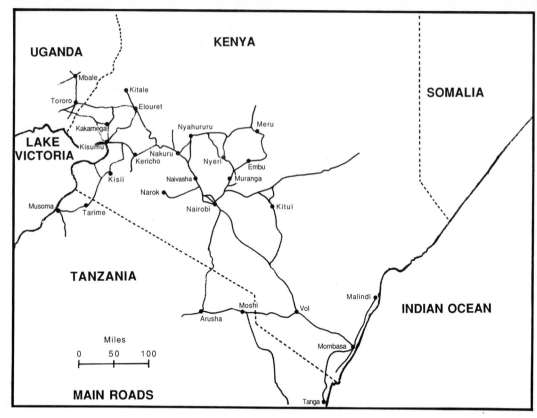

UGANDA

KENYA

SOMALIA

• Mbale
• Kitale
Tororo •
• Elouret
Kakamega •
Nyahururu
• Meru
LAKE
VICTORIA
• Kisumu
• Nakuru
Kericho •
Nyeri •
• Embu
• Kisii
Naivasha •
Muranga •
Narok •
Musoma •
Nairobi
• Kitui
Tarime •

TANZANIA

Malindi •
Moshi •
Vol •
INDIAN OCEAN
Arusha •

Miles

0   50   100

Mombasa •

MAIN ROADS

Tanga •

in a rather attractive yellow/brown/cream in 1977.

In 1984 a new cream/red/black livery was introduced – but this has now been replaced by corporate Stagecoach white.

By the mid-1970s the fleet was becoming fairly standardised. The last four of 33 Guy Arab IV double-deckers new between 1955 and 1957 were withdrawn in 1974 (these four had Park Royal bodies). No Guy Arab single-deckers, Leyland Tigers or Albion Victors remained. Deliveries in the late-1960s had been of Albion Clydesdales and Fiats, plus a few Worldmasters, all except six with local bodies by Labh Singh, Nanak, or Enterprise Road and General Workshops (ERGW). The exceptions were six Fiat 643E with Italian Viberti bodies new in 1965.

Vehicle deliveries in the early-1970s were again Albions and Fiats, the last Fiats, type 331A, were delivered in 1974. Fleet numbers in the 200s, 400s and 600s were reserved by United Transport for East African Road Services (EARS), although a few inter-group transfers retained their numbers. KBS numbers reached 399 by 1969; 500 to 595 were filled up by 1973, while a new series with a new type of vehicle, the Guy Victory, began at 1 in May 1972. By 1979 the Guy fleet had reached 153.

An Ikarus articulated bus was borrowed for a few weeks in late-1975 from Dar es Salaam and was put into service.

In September 1974 the fleet consisted of:

10	Leyland Worldmaster of 1961-68
126	Albion Clydesdale of 1961-71
60	Fiat of 1965-74
81	Guy Victory of 1972-74
277	

By June 1979 the fleet was:

104	Albion Clydesdale
43	Fiat
150	Leyland/Guy Victory
297	

Capacity was generally 47-50 seats with 40-53 standing. Some 13 buses with roof racks were used for private hire or for hire to EARS on country routes – these had around 60 seats and only eight standing spaces.

In 1982 two experimental Isuzu were taken into stock followed in 1983 by a Nissan. Twelve ERFs were delivered between 1986 and 1988. However, most deliveries after 1979 were of Leyland Victory II buses which have an 18ft wheelbase to enable the exit to be located forward of the front axle.

A pair of EARS Guy Victory coaches loading in Nairobi. High-frame chassis with front-mounted engines offer high standards of reliability on indifferent roads. Luggage is carried on the roof.

To round off the picture, the fleet at October 1988 consisted of:

288	Leyland/Guy Victory
11	ERF
2	Isuzu
1	Nissan
302	

KBS ran into serious problems with matatus (minibuses and converted pickups) in the 1970s, which caused a serious drop in the trend of growth of traffic and caused the fleet to remain stable, growing only from 290 in 1975 to 302 in 1988 (with a peak of 316 in 1981 when certain longer suburban routes were being operated).

The population of Nairobi had reached 650,000 by the early-1970s, and since then is said to have almost doubled. The KBS fleet of 300 could not possibly cope with all the demand, as has been proved on occasions when a police blitz on unroadworthy or illegal vehicles has occasionally driven the matatus off the road.

Competition from matatus began on a large scale only after the government in 1973, following an ILO report on employment creation, legalised matatus up to three tons. The number of matatus, which concentrated generally on KBS' core routes, rose from 400 in 1973 to 1,500 in 1977 and later to 2,000. In

EARS adopted the OTC East African fleetname in the late-1970s. This is a 1972 Victory, newly rebodied in 1979 by Labh Singh.

A former United Land & Water Clydesdale running for EARS at Kisumu in 1979. The letters FRI below the cab window indicate that it is to be serviced on Fridays. Small windows and closely-spaced body pillars give added strength in roll-over accidents.

1984 a matatu was legally defined as any vehicle seating up to 25, and purpose-built 25-seat midibuses have increased markedly since then.

Mombasa

Mombasa, an island of some nine square miles, is the largest port on the coast of East Africa. KBS (Mombasa) Ltd began operating in 1936, with seven Albion Victors with Duple bodies.

Services developed gradually and Mombasa Municipal Council purchased 49% of the shares in 1972, United Transport holding the remainder. As in Nairobi, the former United Transport interest is now held by Stagecoach.

Town services are largely confined to Mombasa Island and are operated under a franchise from the Municipal Council. In 1975, 28 million passengers were carried. Country services, running as far as Malindi and Taveta via Voi, in 1975 varied between 30 and 540 kms in length.

A route joint with Tanzanian-based Dar es Salaam Motor Transport Ltd (DMT), later National Bus Services (NBS) or KAMATA, its shortened Swahili name, was operated to Tanga until the border with Tanzania closed in January 1977. Prior to nationalisation DMT was a United Transport subsidiary. KBS (Mombasa) has one large depot in Zanzibar Road, and a bus station-cum-head office block at Mwembe Tayari in the centre of the island was opened in 1966.

The livery had always been cream with a broad green stripe and later two narrower stripes. A new livery of off-white with a red stripe was introduced in the mid-1980s.

As in Nairobi, Guy Arab double-deckers were operated while other vehicles had been Guys, Leylands and Albions of various types.

By 1971 the fleet consisted of nine country buses (Albion Clydesdales) and 52 town buses (mostly Albions with a handful of old Leyland Worldmasters), all with local bodies, most of which were built in Nairobi.

In 1976/7 a new style of body with small windows by Haji Suleiman of Mombasa was introduced on ten Albion Clydesdale CD27s. Two earlier Clydesdales were rebodied with smart new Haji Suleiman coach bodies in 1978/79 for country routes.

In 1978 the fleet was 12 country buses and 70 urban (all Albions). The oldest of these were replaced by 25 Guy Victory IIs in 1979/80, followed by the first ERF Trailblazer bus in 1983. Forty-four ERFs were in service by 1986, replacing most of the remaining Albions.

By the mid-1970s competition from matatus had become serious. In September 1977, 747 matatus were identified by individual registration numbers in a census and the competition was such that serious revenue losses were occurring and the fleet was reduced from 105 to 82. By 1978 matatu numbers were up to 1,277.

KBS (Mombasa) runs two ferries. The ferry operations at Likoni, which also began in 1936, provide the only link to the south coast mainland. Four car ferries are operated on this crossing. There is also a passenger only ferry nearby at Mtongwe which crosses Kilindini Harbour.

Country Buses

The first roads in East Africa were, and most still are, either earth (which means mud when it rains, dust when it's dry) or murram, a surface of gravel which becomes corrugated with ridges at right angles to the road after a few months and then has to be regraded. This takes its toll on country buses.

There are many private or independent operators in Kenya. One of the oldest is East African Road Services of Nairobi.

It has a complicated history beginning in 1947 but, although managed by United Transport, it has been 51% locally owned and quoted on the Nairobi Stock Exchange since June 1971.

A comprehensive network of routes was operated by the 1970s, covering most tarmac roads and not a few miles off-tarmac which still caused considerable problems. The major routes from Nairobi were to Mombasa, to Dar es Salaam via Arusha and Moshi (joint with DMT, later NBS of Tanzania), to Kisumu, to Kisii and Homa Bay, to Kampala in Uganda, and to Kitale. There were also routes from Mombasa to Kitui and to Arusha and from Kisumu to Tarime (in Tanzania). These routes generally involved a day or night service and sometimes both. For example, the Tanzania group of services required six buses (two on night services), while Kampala required eight buses (four on night services).

Of 31 routes operated in 1967, only seven were 100 per cent on tarmac, while three routes from Kisumu (over 100 miles each) were 85 per cent off tarmac. The bad roads, combined with freak weather, sometimes caused serious accidents. A 1967 Albion was swept away in heavy rain on the road to Garissa in 1969. It ended up in quicksand and had to be

A small Fiat 662, setting out from Nairobi on a 100-mile trip to the north. The centre-entrance body has a substantial set of bars ahead of the doorway to protect the panels and windows from heavy luggage being manhandled in and out of the roof rack.

written off. A 1968 Fiat was another coach which suffered by being swept off a bridge in a flash flood on the road to Arusha in 1970. However, it was salvaged.

United Land and Water Transport Co of Kisumu, which was founded by the politician Tom Mboya in 1966, was acquired after his death by EARS in 1970. By 1972 it had 44 buses. It was carried on as a separate subsidiary for a number of years, but ran into financial problems caused by competition and lack of supervision, being so far from Nairobi. The fleet was reduced and the rump of 20 vehicles were repainted into EARS livery in early 1979.

Politics can play a part in African bus operations and 1969 saw the appearance of a firm called Quick Bus Service, whose main shareholder was the wife of the Chief Justice. It quickly acquired a fleet of 30 buses, and, somehow, licences to many routes paralleling EARS routes, with buses in a similar livery. Its intention was to build an 'alternative' to EARS. However, EARS kept its nerve, and Quick slowly faded away.

A factor affecting the issue of licences by the late-1960s was the encouragement of Africanisation and the growing prejudice against foreign-owned companies. To help combat this, EARS offered its shares for sale to the public beginning in 1969, so that by 1971 it was no longer a 'foreign' company.

By 1969 the 300-mile route to Mombasa was suffering competition from licensed Peugeot estate care services. During the year, because of their involvement in so many accidents, their running time was legally increased from six to eight hours. EARS, however, were still limited to 30mph, ie ten hours. Peugeot fares at this time were roughly double those of EARS.

EARS itself took several initiatives towards going upmarket from 1971. In that year the first of a fleet of restyled, more comfortable vehicles known as Safarimaster was introduced on the major routes. A new businessman's express cut one hour off the journey time to Kisumu (210 miles). The 1972 version was updated as the Safarichief.

In 1975 three luxury coaches, with only 40 reclining seats, were placed on the Nairobi-Mombasa service. The advertised fare was 45 shillings for an eight hour journey. (Peugeots took six hours at this time and cost 70 shillings.)

Nakuru town services, which had been acquired by EARS in 1964, were extended in 1969 and revitalised with a new white/orange livery in 1972. Although eight purpose-built standee-type buses were in use by 1975, competition caused the operation to close in December 1976.

An even more serious situation had developed, meanwhile, on the cross-border routes. Although traffic was buoyant, exchange control restrictions, introduced originally in 1970 and 1971, prevented the

Top right:
From the start of the 1970s most Kenyan builders switched to a squarer body style, as shown on this Clydesdale in Kisumu bus station. Under British Leyland's management, Clydesdales were badged as Leylands. This one has 200 miles to go on its trip from Mawingo to Nairobi.

Below right:
Nairobi bus station in 1975, with an Eastern Mbitini Bus Co Clydesdale in the foreground. The Clydesdale was powered by Leyland's 400 engine, which struggled gamely with gross overloads. A loader helps put luggage in the rack of the small Fiat on the left.

money earned in the other territories from being remitted to Nairobi. Eventually, the problems became so serious that EARS was forced to withdraw from the routes to Tanzania in 1975. For similar financial reasons, EARS withdrew from the routes to Uganda in 1976. Some other routes were withdrawn too around this time because of the terrible roads. EARS was hard hit by the loss of revenue from these withdrawals and a number of redundancies were made.

The livery was generally all white until the 1960s, then a broad black band was added. A revised version with two further thin black stripes was introduced in 1970. In 1979 the black was replaced by gold or yellow – in one broad band – but only on new buses.

Although the company tried to use the fleet name East African, it has always been popularly known as OTC, (from the old name Overseas Touring Co). From about 1971 the initials OTC were painted in the front right hand destination box and OTC was always painted in large letters on the rear.

A battered Clydesdale in Nairobi illustrates earlier styles of standard Kenyan bodies, with rounded front and rear domes. Many long-distance buses such as this had three-plus-two seating to maximise carrying capacity.

Buses used on international routes had the words 'Transfer Traffic' prominently painted on each side along the roof rack. Such buses carried two registration numbers, ie Kenya and either Uganda or Tanzania. ULWT buses carried MON, TUE, WED, etc on the front offside to denote the day of the week for servicing!

In the early postwar days Bedfords had been operated by EARS. These were later replaced by Albion Victors and a few Leyland Comets and other makes. From 1960 the standard vehicle was the Albion CD23 Clydesdale, always with local bodies. In 1966 eight Leyland Worldmasters were purchased – some were put on Kampala-Mombasa through workings, a 24-hour journey.

In the mid-1960s 26 Fiat 643E (four with Viberti bodies) were acquired.

By June 1967 the fleet comprised:

13	Leyland Worldmaster
14	Fiat
50	Albion Clydesdale CD23
—	
77	
—	

Small batches of other types – seven Albion CD31s in 1969, eight South African-built Leyland Elands in 1971, and four truck-derived Leyland Lynxes in 1974 – were taken in. All other purchases until 1974, apart from two Guy Victories in 1972, were Clydesdale CD23s. Then the fleet was standardised on the Guy Victory.

The fleet was expanded to 122 at June 1975 in a burst of optimism but slashed to 77 by June 1977 and 63 by August 1978.

At January 1979 the fleet consisted of:

35	Albion CD23
28	Guy Victory
—	
63	
—	

Bodies have always been locally built, usually in Nairobi by Nanak or Labh Singh, and from 1972 a rather square type had replaced earlier rounded versions.

In 1978 two vehicles received experimental new style bodies, one by Labh Singh and one by Haji Suleiman of Mombasa. The Haji Suleiman bodies were deemed a success and more were ordered for new Victories in 1979.

In 1982 a completely different design of body by Coachworks Ltd, Mombasa, was put into service. These have black window surrounds and a more streamlined look – without the roofracks, which have been replaced by underfloor luggage space.

Private Operators

Some of the independent operators in Kenya are quite substantial, with up to 50 or more vehicles, although there is intense competition on most routes and some of the bigger operators collapsed in the 1970s. It would be a fair generalisation to say that the bus operating situation in Kenya is somewhat fluid. There is a Transport Licensing Act, but you will not find a monopoly on any route. New operators spring up, not always licensed initially, and old operators go bankrupt.

After independence, licences tended to be given to African operators, rather than European or Asian ones. Many African-sounding companies in fact turn out to be owned by Asians.

The area in a radius of 20 miles from Nairobi tends to be served by a particularly large number of small operators and mini-buses, and competition is such that new operators spring up constantly.

One of the most interesting operators is Coast Bus of Mombasa who operate a real mixture of scruffy local routes around Mombasa and luxury long distance sleeping coaches to Nairobi, Kisumu and, formerly, Kampala. Their Albion coaches were cream/green or cream/green/red.

Another significant firm is Akamba Public Road Services of Machakos, 42 miles northeast of Nairobi, which operated from Nairobi to Mombasa and Kampala. Akamba was the first independent on the Nairobi-Kampala route in early-1969. Their buses were all Leyland Albions. Like Coast Bus, an extensive parcel service is operated.

The great majority of vehicles in small fleets in the 1970s came from the Leyland stable — Albion Clydesdale, a few Vikings and Leyland Comets.

Both Leyland and Fiat set up plants for local assembly of bus chassis in 1976 and 1977 and while Leyland was already strong, Fiat increased its share from that date — but mostly with smaller operators.

Some Bedford and Isuzu were assembled at the local General Motors factory, and Mercedes buses were also to be found among the smaller operators.

Bodies were always built in Kenya (although Coast Bus had one Plaxton-bodied vehicle). A major builder in the 1960s was Enterprise Road & General Workshop (ERGW), but this company ceased to manufacture in 1975. Its proprietors sold up and left the country. Labb Singh Harnam Singh was founded in 1928 and built buses for home and export — a major customer being United Transport for its subsidiaries in Kenya, Uganda and Tanzania.

Nanak Body Builders, founded in 1960, was also a major builder for the UT group. Nanak also pioneered luxury coaches for Coast Bus.

Haji Suleman Haji Ladha & Sons of Mombasa and Dar es Salaam gained a larger share of the market from 1977 with its Malaika luxury bodies with underfloor luggage area.

Until the break up of the East African Community in 1976/77, several of these firms built buses for Tanzania and even Zambia. Since then, export orders have been largely for Uganda and Rwanda.

FRESH NEW LOOK

The 1940s and 1950s saw bus makers follow the lead given by car manufacturers in hiding the radiator behind a stylised grille. **Roy Marshall** illustrates different approaches to the new look.

Midland Red was one of Britain's most innovative operators and during World War 2 developed a new style front to hide the radiator on its own-build chassis. This new style was also applied to a batch of 100 AEC Regent IIs delivered between 1948 and 1950, including this Metro-Cammell-bodied bus.
ALL PHOTOS BY ROY MARSHALL.

All postwar Fodens had concealed radiators, hidden behind a flamboyant grille which was also used on the company's truck cabs. Between 1948 and 1956 Warrington Corporation purchased 15 Fodens. This East Lancs-bodied PVD6 dates from 1949.

Right:
Birmingham City Transport followed Midland Red's lead with an attractively styled bonnet and grille assembly which was supplied on Daimler, Guy and, as illustrated here, Crossley chassis. By having a narrow bonnet - unlike the full-width designs used by Midland Red and Foden - the Birmingham front gave drivers a better view of the kerb. Birmingham also fitted attractive wheeltrims to further enhance the appearance of its new buses.

Right:
The Birmingham-style bonnet was adopted as standard by Daimler and as an option by Guy. Only four years separate these two Coventry Corporation Metro-Cammell-bodied Daimlers but the leading bus, a CVD6 photographed when new in 1952, looks infinitely more modern. The polished strip above the grille carried on the Daimler tradition of a fluted top tank on its bus and car radiators.

Below:
Guys with the new-look front were distinguishable from Daimlers only by the badging. Darlington Corporation's first buses with concealed radiators were eight Roe-bodied Arab IIIs delivered in 1954.

Top right:
The Birmingham style was used briefly by AEC and fitted to small numbers of Regent IIIs, including 15 for South Wales Transport in 1954 which had 53-seat lowbridge Weymann bodies.

Bottom right:
Dennis, too, copied the Birmingham style for 32 Lance K4s for Aldershot & District. A&D was the only buyer of Dennis Lances with concealed radiators. East Lancs bodied this example, seen in Reading.

Leyland supplied a batch of Titans with tin
fronts - as the new look was often unkindly
called - to Midland Red in 1952-53 and then
offered the sheet metal grille as an option for
the rest of the 1950s. The shaped area at the
top of the grille was designed to
accommodate Midland Red's BMMO badge -
BMMO being the abbreviation of the
company's full title, the Birmingham &
Midland Motor Omnibus Co. North Western
operated ten Weymann-bodied PD2s with
concealed radiators.

For the Regent V, AEC designed an attractive
new grille which incorporated the triangular
AEC badge. It was long-lived, appearing in
1954 and surviving with little modification
until the end of Regent production in 1968.
King Alfred of Winchester operated this ex-
AEC demonstration Regent V with Park Royal
body.

When Bristol started production of its revolutionary low-frame Lodekka, it featured a concealed radiator with a grille which was in effect a stylised form of the radiator shape used on the previous generation of K-series chassis. Early vehicles had a full-depth grille surround as on this 1954 Mansfield District LD6G in Nottingham.

The Lodekka grille was quickly modified with the lower edge of the surround running above instead of below the square number plate. The front wings were also shortened to improve brake cooling. A 1958 Scottish Omnibuses LD6G in Glasgow illustrates the difference.

When Dennis started building low-frame chassis under licence from Bristol it adopted the Lodekka bonnet but with a distinctive Dennis grille. Middlesbrough Corporation bought one Northern Counties-bodied Loline in 1958, with more following in 1960.

Left:
The first prototype London Transport Routemaster had the radiator mounted under the floor, dispensing with the need for a cooling grille of any sort at the front of the bus. LT's designers took advantage of this freedom to design a simple and attractive front end.

Below:
New-look fronts were rare on single-deckers (apart from Fodens) because the adoption of concealed radiators came at a time when old-style front-engined single-deck chassis were being rendered obsolete by a new generation of underfloor-engined models. This Crossley of Haper Bros of Heath Hayes was rebodied by them in 1959 using MetSec frames. A Guy front end added a touch of modernity.

DURHAM DELIGHTS

Michael Fowler turns the clock back 20 years, to a visit made to County Durham in the summer of 1974.

Above:
Bond Bros of Willington operated AEC Reliances with Plaxton Highway bus bodies. A 1966 example stands outside the company's garage. Bond Bros still operates local services.
ALL PHOTOS BY MICHAEL FOWLER.

Left:
Gillett Bros was one of a number of small operators which took advantage of the government's grant towards the cost of new buses to update its fleet in the 1970s. This Willowbrook-bodied Bedford YRT arriving in Bishop Auckland has a two-person crew.

Gillett Bros also bought new heavyweights. A pair of Plaxton-bodied Reliances were delivered in 1974; one loads in Durham for Hartlepool. Gillett Bros was taken over by United Automobile Services in 1974.

Left:
Trimdon Motor Services ran a large fleet of Fords, which was gradually being replaced by Leyland Leopards in 1974. A 1971 R192 with Willowbrook body stands at Spennymoor. TMS operated 50 buses in 1974. It disappeared in 1990, being absorbed by United. A United RE stands in the background.

Right:
Gypsy Queen, since 1989 a subsidiary of Go-Ahead Northern, with contrasting styles of Bedford YRQ coaches at its Langley Park base. That nearest the camera has a Duple Viceroy body. Alongside stands a Plaxton Panorama Elite.

Above:
The depot of Shaw Bros at Byers Green with an ex-Lancashire United PD3 in the foreground and a smart Plaxton-bodied AEC Reliance of 1964 in the background. The PD3 has a permanently-painted destination display. Shaw Bros was acquired by United in 1975.

OK Motor Services, then as now a major operator in the county, operated Leyland Leopard coaches on local services. This 11m PSU3 in Spennymoor bus station has an early example of Duple's Dominant body.

126

Left
Weardale Motor Services operated this forward-entrance Alexander-bodied Leyland Titan PD3, an unusual choice for a small operator in 1959. Note the registration, 6BUP - most buses bought new by Weardale had 'six' in their registrations. This Titan served the company for over 20 years.

Below:
Another user of the popular Bedford/Willowbrook combination was Diamond Bus Service of Stanley. A 1972 YRQ, which was to run until the end of the 1980s, waits in central Durham. In 1974 Diamond was the trading name of two small family businesses, Hammel and Mowbray. The latter ceased in the 1980s and the Diamond business is now run by the Hammel family.

A later Weardale double-decker was this 1970 Leeds-style Atlantean, a long-wheelbase PDR2 model with dual-door Roe body. It was registered GUP6H and was the company's last new double-decker. Like the PD3 before it, the Atlantean was long-lived, running for 20 years.

Eden Bus Services of West Auckland is another of the County Durham independents which survives 20 years on. In 1974 this Plaxton-bodied Tiger Cub was running on its Spennymoor service. It was new to Weardale.

United, part of the National Bus Company, was a major provider of services in the north east. Among the more interesting buses in its fleet was this ex-Western SMT Bristol VRT, photographed in Bishop Auckland. It was acquired by United when the Scottish Bus Group decided to rid itself of VRTs which were proving unreliable in service.